the SALTIMBANQUE REVIEW

Number One

the SALTIMBANQUE REVIEW

Number One

Saltimbanque Books

New York

The cover image was created by the
Donaldson Litho. Co., Newport, KY, in 1900.

Book typeset and designed by Christopher Boynton

Saltimbanque Books, New York
www.saltimbanquebooks.com

ISBN: 978-1-941914-09-0

TABLE OF CONTENTS

the

SALTIMBANQUE REVIEW

Number One

Killing: A Primer

Matt Tanner

She said to put them in a sack—yelled it from the kitchen as you chased one through the yard, then again when you tried to bring one inside—but when you look under the kitchen sink all you find is a crumpled brown grocery bag, so you decide to put the writhing kittens in that. You tramp around the outside of the house, the blood still hot in your cheeks from being slapped. Under the bushes behind the garage, they bound and swat at each other, bouncing and rolling in the pine straw, but eventually you catch each one in your ten-year-old fingers, hoisting them between elbow and shoulder as you hold the bag open on the ground with your free hand.

You trudge in the heat through the dry grass toward the woods, holding the bag from beneath and staring in at the kittens, almost tripping in the kudzu that has crept over the back quarter of the yard. You step into the shade and slip down the embankment and walk rock-to-rock upstream until you reach the shallow pool. You sit on a large rock and dangle your feet in the creek, the bag on your lap. The kittens look up at you with their oversized eyes. The orange one you call Tiger stands on his back legs and scratches at the paper wall of the worn bag, and you take him out and pet him, and he begins to purr, a sound you can't hear over the creek's babble but can feel through your hand. After a moment you drop him back into the bag and wade out into the creek, the water licking at your thighs and wicking up the frayed ends of your cutoffs. You roll closed the opening and push the bag into the water.

Years later—perhaps carrying a stolen television into a pawn shop or lifting weights on the concrete slab on a lawn behind razor wire—you'll realize that what you really needed was a pillow case and a couple good rocks, a brick maybe. But here in the chill of the creek and the thick air of summer, the bag is coming apart. The kittens have torn a hole through the paper.

One by one, they rise and surface and drift in the stream. A black one sinks its claws into your forearm, and you shake it off and splash downstream to catch two others bobbing in the current. One is Tiger, the other a tiny calico no one's named, but they are no longer the teensy animals you played with earlier in the day. Their teeth are needles; their claws, razors. Your arms are streaked with fine parallel lines that sting in the water. The calico champs down with its tiny mouth on your thumb, and you fling it away, and then there's just Tiger. You push him under and hold him there. He twists and burbles in the water, monstering your hands until, finally, he stops and you let go.

Tiger's body floats away in the current, and you shiver in the cold water, glad to no longer be close to something dead. You begin gulping breath after breath in the stillness, your eyes moist, your nose dripping snot. What is left of the bag clings to a stone. For a moment your ears buzz, but then there's another sound: the kittens have reached a bend a few feet downstream and have come ashore, mewing, their voices a malevolent chorus.

Supper with the Exorcist

Brian Hurley

A SKITTISH CLUTCH

After forty-some years of ho-hum, every-other-Sunday churchgoing, my father decided one morning—after he accidentally knocked the Oldsmobile into reverse and collided with a cypress tree near the driveway, pulling his eventual death into sudden focus—to devote his life to God. He became a deacon at our Lutheran church, which meant he could assist the pastor by giving sermons, presiding at weddings and funerals, and preparing the altar for sacraments.

I called my father by his first name, Gary, because I was sixteen and all bets were off.

Gary acted like my mom and I would never understand his sacred duties—the weekly visits to the sick, the evening naps with a Bible on his lap—when in fact we understood him all too well. He was growing a beard and reading the early Roman theologians as if he had found the key to a happier existence. It was just like the time Gary built a greenhouse and said we would grow our own vegetables from now on. Or the time he took all those nude photos of my mom and mailed them to art galleries.

THE GREENHOUSE DIDN'T PAN OUT

Five minutes into a supper of beef lasagna and canned vegetables, the phone rang. "It's Louise," my mom said, "from the pastor's office. She says you need to get down there right away."

"What happened?"

"Something is wrong with Ray Stoudamire."

A chair squealed as Gary pushed away from the table.

Car keys flashed in his hand. I was desperate to drive the Oldsmobile. As soon as Gary poked his arm through his coat sleeve, I snatched the keys. He spun around, fists clenched, as if he intended to fight me. But when he saw my mother, he relaxed his jaw, and his shoulders rolled back.

"Tell Louise we'll be there in ten minutes."

WE ALMOST CRASH

I was cruising through a perfectly legal, yellow stoplight, when a Dodge pickup jumped out of the intersection to my right. An instant later I braked, but I had already swerved into the oncoming lane. For a second I locked eyes with an elderly woman behind the wheel of a black Honda. Our fenders almost kissed. There was no crash, but I felt a phantom impact in the soles of my feet. It rippled through my body and collapsed my lungs like a deck of shuffled cards.

Gary was so busy reading his deacon's manual that he barely noticed. He just gripped the door handle and leaned slightly to the right.

I drove on to the church.

THE ONLY LIGHT CAME FROM THE BELLTOWER. PIGEONS USED TO ROOST UP THERE UNTIL THE CROWS CAME AND SCARED THEM OFF. THEN WE LAID SPIKES ON ALL THE RIDGES AND ARCHWAYS TO DRIVE THE CROWS AWAY. WE COULD ABIDE THE PIGEONS BUT NOT THE CROWS. THAT ALWAYS BOTHERED ME. ACTUALLY, THERE WAS A SECOND LIGHT COMING FROM THE CHURCH—I SAW A CANDLE FLICKERING IN THE SANCTUARY. THE CHURCH WAS GUARDED BY THICK WOODEN DOORS, BUT GARY HAD KEYS TO A SIDE ENTRANCE.

Gary entered the church.

I pulled over and let the engine run.

GHOSTS IN OUTER SPACE

The sky overhead was cloudless and black. I watched it through my windshield as if it were moving.

Constellations and visible planets used to be a source of wonder and comfort for me, until my father, on a kick about space exploration, explained why the stars appear to blink. He said a million gaseous particles are drifting before our eyes, totally invisible, and when they pass in front of the stars they obscure our vision for a moment. He said I should think of these particles as ghosts in outer space. And then he gave a low, hideous laugh.

Since then, I have tried my hardest not to believe in ghosts. Even now, I prefer my night skies cloudy.

ST. THOMAS WAS A DOUBTER

Gary came out and stood by the driver's side window. "Okay," he said. "It's an exorcism." He was tugging the sharp bristles of his beard so hard I thought his face might come off. I wanted him to rip it away, like a mask, toss it on the seat beside me, and say, "Fuck it, let's get the hell out of here." And I would throw his door open and we would peel away like bank robbers. But he just stood there and stroked his beard.

"Stars are out," he said.

And then we heard a sickening scream. The lights behind a stained glass of St. Thomas flared out, briefly, and snapped back on. I may have been old enough to drive, but I was still young enough to feel my ribcage seize up when I was afraid.

"What's going on?"

Gary said, "Ray Stoudamire came to the pastor's office this morning, and I guess he just lost control. Freaked out. Pastor

Evan is in there right now, trying to calm him down. I'm supposed to sit with them and pray. That's supposed to help." Gary looked pale. "Do me a favor. Circle the block if you want, but stay close. I'll come back if I need you."

"Need me for what?" I started to say, but I couldn't find the breath.

Gary disappeared into the church. I rolled forward and parked beside a chain link fence. As soon as I killed the engine, I felt something in my chest throw a little fit, and I dropped my forehead on the steering wheel.

WHO IS RAY STOUDAMIRE?

He belonged to our church, but I never would have known him if my father wasn't a deacon. Ray lived in a homeless shelter, and he came to Sunday services with the fervor of the newly converted. He served coffee, shook hands with all the ladies, and made the sign of the cross before touching the collection plate. I, on the other hand, was born into the church, so there was no cause for excitement. In a ten-block radius of the steeple I had my school, a baseball diamond, a comic book store, and a lonely stretch of road where the older kids raced their cars at night. That was my whole life.

THE SANCTUARY

I pictured Ray Stoudamire strapped to the altar while Gary and Pastor Evan sliced his chest open with a blessed knife, and all the demons, or whatever, came flying out. I thought of sharp fangs and secret incantations and chamber pots swirling with blood. I knew my head would explode at the sight of such unfathomable gore. Somehow it was even worse being on my own, in the Oldsmobile, under a night sky.

So I entered the church.

Ray Stoudamire was slumped beneath the baptismal font, a mixture of anger and confusion streaked across his face like tracks in the mud. The sanctuary was quiet except for the brush of Pastor Evan's loafers on the carpet. He wore a gray sweatshirt from his alma mater as he paced the central aisle. I wasn't scared like I thought I would be.

But the screaming, when it came again, was like the cry of a cornered dog. It leaped from Ray Stoudamire's throat in staccato bursts that broke and re-broke the silence of the wooden rafters. His body wrenched into action and he climbed to his feet. That's when Pastor Evan stepped forward and pinned him down. Shaking and shuddering, he brought Ray back to earth. It seemed like such an arbitrary struggle—one man goes up, the other goes down—but it felt like all hell would break loose if Ray ever made it to his feet.

I recognized my father in the first pew, his shoulders locked in concentration, his head bowed in prayer. When he saw me running toward him, his eyes melted like candles, and I saw his surprise, fear and determination dripping down. With his cheeks breaking out in something like a sweat, he hustled us both outside, to the Oldsmobile, and we got back on the road.

HOW THE DEMONS CAME TO POSSESS RAY STOUDAMIRE

Apparently Ray went to a free clothing drive at the homeless shelter, and they gave him a new coat. He said the demons were in the coat. As soon as he pulled it on, they entered his body.

I said I didn't believe it. Gary said neither did he, but the important thing was that Ray believed it.

A COLD LASAGNA SUPPER WITH THE EXORCIST

The road home was slick and dazzled by street lamps.

“Use your turn signal,” Gary said. “Go a little further before you start the turn. Right here is good.” Each time he opened his mouth I knew exactly what he was going to say, but I didn’t stop him.

Gary said, “Did you get enough to eat before we left?”

I shook my head.

“We’ll fix you something.”

Turnpike

Heather Austin

Ray asked me to marry him in the K-Mart parking lot after I got out of work. When I saw him waiting for me by my car, I pulled off my red vest with the fake nametag that read "Lola" with a Pooh bear sticker next to it, and hoped he didn't notice it. The lot was full of puddles that reflected the sign with the burned-out A. I figured that they would have fixed it sooner if it had been the K that burned out. When he opened the box, the ring nestled in black velvet glistened under the bright parking lot light.

"It's lovely," I said. This had happened once before with a boy named Alex when I was pregnant and sixteen. It had been easier to say yes back then.

"I'll answer tomorrow." I pushed the ring back at him.

"Give me your keys," he said. He slipped the band onto my key ring next to a Corona bottle opener. "Take it off when you're ready."

So far three men have wanted to marry me, but I only said yes to Alex who died a week later in a car accident. I'd think about him being dead but I couldn't picture him. He kept turning into other people who I wouldn't really mind being dead. I tried to remember what he smelled like and how he felt underneath me as I kneeled over him in the backseat of his Jeep. His favorite ice cream was pralines and cream and I miscarried his child. My family said he is why I can never settle down. It was just easier to tell them they were right.

The next morning Ray woke me up before he left for work. "I need you to run this into the city for me." He tapped his finger on his manuscript.

"Fedex it," I said, and pulled the comforter over my head. Usually I slept well into the afternoon when I stayed over.

"I want you to go, it might inspire you."

At the Wantagh station, a woman asked me for a cigarette

and luckily I had some because I was wearing Ray's jacket, a long German army coat from the thrift store that smelled like some other man. I quit smoking when I was fifteen.

I gave her a Dunhill and she said, "I hate these cigarettes. Do you want to share a seat on the train?" Her name was Ellen and she insisted on the window seat and on leaning in real close when she spoke. She was wire-thin and smelled hot, like fire. She told me she was hit by lightning at a church picnic when she was nine. It hadn't even been raining. I can't decide whether I thought she smelled like that before or after she told me the story.

When we changed at Jamaica, she wrote her number in black pen on the palm of my hand. As she drew a heart around it, I told her Ray wanted to marry me.

"You're young! What about college?" Ellen said, squinting her black-rimmed eyes.

"*College?*" I said and laughed.

"I'm in my last year of law school, I know what you mean."

I told her Ray taught at my old high school, but it isn't his real job. "He's got a novel coming out." I patted the marked-up galleys in my bag.

"I don't have time for fiction," Ellen said.

"Neither do I."

Later that week Ray and I had another fight about school, about the ring. After the shouting was over he sat at his kitchen table with a stack of bad high school poems next to his elbow and said, "You really ought to think about what you're doing with your life. You don't even write anymore."

I opened a can of beer. I thought of my $6.75 an hour job, my old Volkswagen hatchback, and Ellen. She was waiting for me at the Turnpike Diner.

"I'm doing all right," I said. I pushed the tab of the can back and forth.

"Exactly," he said and then picked up his coffee cup and started grading the papers. He left a ring of coffee on the first page. I hated when teachers did that.

"You should go," he said. "I can't look at you right now."

At the diner I told Ellen everything while we waited for our coffee.

She stacked the half and halfs into a pyramid as she listened. Her fingers had big knuckles that she cracked after making a point.

"What an asshole. At least he didn't say *you should write a poem about this.*"

I held my head. "He did."

Our waiter set down our coffees. His black ponytail was coming undone.

"Bob, you're the best," I said.

Ellen eyed his nametag. "Why do you call him Bob?"

"Because he lets me."

Ellen and I began meeting up on Fridays at the diner after going out with our separate friends and talked until I was sober enough to drive home. If Ellen was late, Bob and I smoked a joint in the Men's restroom and talked about his wife. If Ellen was early, she put two dollars' worth of quarters in the juke box, enough to play Blondie's "One Way Or Another" four times.

She always had a negative revelation about Ray. "You know he only smokes Dunhills to impress women," she said, waving an imported Sobranie of her own.

I always thought it was because of Hunter S. Thompson but I shrugged and said, "That explains everything."

Ellen's boyfriend Dave was a manager at the CVS I used to steal lipstick from in eighth grade. I took thirty-seven in all, every color that Almay had out that year, and some duplicates. I don't think I wore any of them.

Ellen was graduating third in her class at Columbia Law. Dave said he was fine with Ellen's success. He was sort of sad and blond and wanted to someday be a painter. I wondered if I was Ray's Dave.

"Do you ever think of marrying Dave?" I asked her as I rubbed the engagement ring on my key chain. I didn't know if it was for luck or penitence.

"No," she said, startled by the question, and I wondered if I should have been startled by questions of marriage too.

"Are you going to leave Ray or marry him?" Ellen asked. She picked a strand of hair from her lip and waited a long time for my answer.

I never know if I am going to leave or stay, I never know until the moment just before. My first boyfriend was the color of coffee. He taught me how to sing from the center of my stomach. When I think of music I think of him and of the bitter taste of his sweat. He asked me to marry him a month after I met him. I told him he was crazy, we were only fifteen. He said I was afraid of what people would think. Ellen liked to hear stories about him because he sometimes played guitar at the coffee house she went to with her other friends. I made a point never to go there.

I left him and became best friends with a girl who wrote stories instead of songs. She had long dark hair and thought she was prettier then she was. We were good friends for a long, long time, and sometimes I forget that Ellen is not her.

This summer, the summer after everyone else's freshman year at college, I ended up spending the weekends going to parties at their houses, drinking their beer, and pretending not to notice how much they hadn't changed. In the fall they'll be gone again, and some have already left—packing their cars full of down comforters, CDs, and bongs. It won't be as hard watching them leave this time, and Ellen said that's a good thing.

At least once at each keg party I was asked if it was true that I'm engaged to Mr. Banks, our old high school English teacher. I told them, "We're figuring things out." I didn't tell them how Ray started talking about his new student Carrie Jackson's poems the way he used to talk about mine.

At a party in Long Beach, where I didn't even go to high school, I had to refute a rumor that Ray got me pregnant. Afterwards a boy named Steve who I knew junior year came up to me, high on E, and put his arm around my shoulders.

He leaned his damp forehead against mine and said, "I used to write you poems."

I told him, "Ray J. Banks writes better ones, although not to me."

I left the party early and sober, and I drove without thinking to the diner. The rain was coming down so hard I almost missed the left on Hempstead Turnpike. The pink neon sign streaked across my windshield as I pulled into the parking lot.

"You look down, let's go get cheered up," Bob said when I came in the door. My hair was wet from the rain and I smoothed it back and nodded. I followed him into the handicapped stall and smoked while I waited for Ellen to show up.

The walls in there were gray tile and covered in black marker sex poems. We sat on the floor and leaned our heads together as we passed the joint. Tattoos snaked up his forearm from when he was in the Marines. When he told me he was dishonorably discharged, I didn't ask what for. He said that's what he liked about me.

"Do you mind?" he said, and touched his hand to my knee.

I didn't, so he rested his hand there, rubbing my skin through the hole in my jeans.

"Tell me things," he said.

My mother worked the night shift the winter I turned fourteen. Some of the popular girls from school used to come over while she was out. We smoked her cigarettes in my room, listened to Nirvana, and put on enough eyeliner to get into R-rated movies. Sometimes boys showed up and they'd try to make out with us in my living room with the lights on. They kissed too hard; we could feel their teeth behind the softness of their lips. Their faces pressed into ours with urgency as if they needed to make our mouths theirs.

During that year I got a reputation and my best friend Jen Miller got an abortion. She whispered the secret to me in gym class, while we huddled behind the bike shed smoking cigarettes instead of playing tennis. I took a puff and said, "I guess that means you're going to hell, but least you don't have to walk around this shithole pregnant."

She agreed, and then told me she decided to start doing acid instead of guys because it made her feel like she finally understood something.

Ellen was Drug Free. She took prescription medicine for her sinuses and *that's it*. Her boyfriend told her nicotine is a drug but she won't hear it. I like to drink wine in long-stemmed glasses. My mother drinks vodka straight, which even the smell of makes me vomit. She told me once that my father was a beer man and by the time he was thirty he had a belly you could rest a cup on. She also says that about my hips. I once went to a bar that he used to go to and did seven whiskey shots in a row. Later, in the back of the bar, I gave a hand job to a stranger who afterward stiffed me with his bill.

I touched Bob's hand on my knee. "Why don't you wear a wedding ring? Is it so you can cheat on your wife?"

He jumped, burning himself with the joint, and sucked on his finger.

"Come here, run it under the tap." I took him over to the sink. I held his hand under the water until my fingers felt numb from the cold.

"We couldn't afford rings. I've never cheated on her," he said. I could feel him though, hard against me as we leaned over the sink. He realized it too and pulled away.

"It's not a serious burn, you'll be fine," I said. I felt bad for him then. "I'm glad we smoked that joint. I need to get the munchies to eat the crap you serve me," I said, and he laughed.

"Where were you?" Ellen asked as I slid into our booth.

"With Bob."

"He likes you, be careful." She was wearing too much black makeup and the rain had smeared it around her eyes. Her skin was pale and perfect. She looked like a death mask of herself.

"Have you ever been so scared you felt like you were going to die?" I asked suddenly. I can't think of anything appropriate to say when I'm high.

"Well there was that time I was hit by lightning," she said. "What about you?" She tore open a packet of Sugar Twin.

Every month I'm afraid. I think of children and the blood that rushed down my thighs when I tripped down the stairs at the mall when I was sixteen. I tried to catch the blood in my hands, wiping it up off the floor and bringing it to myself, trying to push it back inside me. A middle-aged woman dropped her Nordstrom's shopping bag and kneeled next to me at the bottom of the stairs. The bag opened up and her clothes scattered across the floor. Without saying anything she took a blue silk shirt and cleaned off my hands. She held my head as I rocked back and forth in pain until the ambulance came.

My mother said it was a blessing. Some people said I did it on purpose. My shoes got covered with blood, and they're still in my closet, the leather ruined.

"One decaf and one regular," Bob said, and placed our coffees in front of us, startling me.

"I've never been afraid," I answered Ellen. I reached for my cup and accidentally spilled my coffee on the table. She mopped it up with her sleeve and grabbed my hand.

"I saw Ray downtown today. Catch this—he was with Carrie Jackson. He was smoking Marlboros so she can collect more miles. She's saving them for a fucking Marlboro red tent so she can go camping in Jersey. She actually said *Jersey*," Ellen said and flicked her ashes. They landed outside of the ashtray.

"That explains everything," I said, cracking my knuckles. "Put on some Blondie."

"Atta girl." Ellen smiled and flipped through the jukebox pages loudly, even though she has the number memorized. Before we left, I wrote a note for Bob on my napkin—"For your wife"— and placed my engagement ring on top as a tip.

Occasional

— for Katherine

go where I cannot
but hide from me
a fossil containing as many
as seven crystal spirals
or more   of song
goodbye's melody : a local echo's
white notes to plume the sometimes
green air

then move
into yourself
some few things: quartzy
Bronx nights far from the vast

compression of Manhattan
admonitions of a well traveled

thesaurus   unanswerable
questions pulled like a handkerchief
from the empty fist
of a hand you held

—Douglas Hahn

Lion

Amy Roa

This whole shit went down the night I was looking for that fat kid Lino, cuz I lent him my bolt cutters, but I was wanting my bolt cutters back to steal this bike some dumbass left chained outside the YMCA. I got the fag song on me, YMCA, YMCA, why don't you stay at the YMCA, getting me irritated and I'm for real thinking about stabbing the fat kid with the YMCA song singing inside me.

I get to the fat kid's building and outside I find him eating a lion. He's got his mouth open wide on the lion's fur. So I tell the fat fuck, that's a real dope lion. He tells me yeah, and it's real too.

The lion's small enough to lay down on the fat kid's lap having its fur rubbed. The fat kid won't stop shooting out the tears and I knock him one on the head but that doesn't do shit, and I knock him one more with my Timberlands and he's got a heel mark on his forehead and that surprises the fuck out of him. He tells me, ouch, and that he couldn't stop them from killing his lion. I tell him I'm real pissed off to see this lion dead. I tell him what he kill it for, that if I knew the fat kid was the lion killing type of guy I wouldn't have lent him my bolt cutters. I knock him one more with my Timberlands, I tell him that one was for the lions that can't do shit for themselves, the helpless "I'm just here hanging with my pride of lions." The dead lion's stretched out with its head on its paws and its feet tucked in behind it. It's getting me way reflective thinking about those assholes in jeeps that gang up on elephants to get at their ivory and make piano keys and ivory toilet plungers and shit. The fat kid doesn't know I watch nature shows and that I think all the shit that goes on in the jungle to tigers, elephants, apes, gazelles and everybody else is fucked up or else he wouldn't have been chilling with the dead lion that isn't even near being full grown right in my face. He tells me he didn't touch the lion.

That his moms and pops threw it out the window and that he's real sad about it, like messed up sad about it, and he's thinking of doing some stuff to himself now that he doesn't have a pet lion. I kneel down to get a close up look at the lion. If the fat fuck hadn't told me it was dead I would've jumped him for it, taken it home and tried to raise it until my moms called me a shithead for bringing a dead lion into her place with its death stink. Don't be telling me those things, I tell the fat fuck. I tell him he could get the lion stuffed. It's a real good-looking lion so I reach over and pet its brown spots. It's a warm, fresh lion. The fat fuck tells me he lives on the eighth floor and I look up to the windows of his building and have to hold on to my stomach cuz I've got this picture of a lion falling and I'm not into heights.

The fat fuck tells me he's been waiting for someone to walk by and take a look at this lion, and that he closed its eyes right before I got there, and that his lion needs a vet, and could I help get his lion to a vet.

What the fuck good would it do, I tell the fat fuck. He tells me he was just chilling here when the lion fell out the window.

The fat fuck spends some time hauling up the lion to show me how big it'd got eating four chickens a day and lots of milk, so I finally get sick of it and tell him to lift with his knees. He tells me it was way smaller when he got it, and that he was a good father to the lion.

There's no blood on it. It's a good-looking lion, I tell the fat fuck as a way of looking on the good side of the dead lion with us.

Oh man, oh man, oh man, the fat fuck tells me using his head to pet the lion. He tells me, why am I so stupid, and that the blood's bleeding on the inside, man, and what am I gonna do about it now.

But see, I'm not comfortable with this shit. This isn't what I was looking for, so I just tell the fat fuck I need my bolt cutters so I can bounce out of there and think about good things once I have that dude's bike that's sitting outside the YMCA. And that, shit, if he wanted I could let him use it for a week or so before I have to spray paint it and sell it off. The fat fuck starts crying for me not to stab him like I told him I would if he didn't have my bolt cutters, but he can't remember where he put my bolt cutters but he's for sure they're upstairs. I tell the fat fuck this isn't his day, and I'm pissed. I'm just a young dude looking for his bolt cutters to steal a bike and put some money in his pocket. But that night I found a dead lion laying by a fat fuck I'd known since the fourth grade. The fat fuck's looking at me like I'm the real goddamned Jesus Christ come down to chill with him and his dead lion, maybe even lay my hands on him and make a miracle. I tell the fat fuck the look he's giving me doesn't make me feel joyous and that his ass better get upstairs and look for my bolt cutters or I was gonna do the deed with this swiss army knife I had in my pocket. The fat fuck didn't burn one calorie cuz he didn't move. I tell him, what's moving look like, man. He tells me his moms and pops are up there, and that they killed his lion. He starts shaking and I tell him if he's having a seizure or something. He tells me he's okay, it's just his body. The fat fuck's scared and everything has to be gotten done by me alone, man. The fat fuck tells me his apartment number and I'm out.

The lady opens the door wearing a shirt with no panties and I tell her hey, I'm Jesus, Lino's friend. She tells me Lino isn't home yet. I tell her yeah, he's sitting outside with his dead lion. She tells me, huh. Then she asks me if I want a beer and doesn't bother to cover her ass with her shirt when she walks away to get me that beer. While she's away I sit myself down next to this man watching one of my favorite shows. I tell him hey, I'm Jesus, just like I did the lady and he starts shooting tears just like the fat fuck offspring. He tells me he's sorry and don't look at him. So I don't. The lady comes back with my beer and I look at her snatch. I'm sitting on these couch cushions on the floor between this man and this lady just like they were my own moms and pops, watching TV together, kind of real after-school special except for that they murdered a lion. These were the fat fuck's parents. This was lion country. There was one fucked-up mattress on the floor and a smaller one by the window. There was a baby bottle the lion sucked on, and newspapers the lion pissed on. I start thinking about how am I gonna stab the fat fuck when I was only faking about having a swiss army knife, and don't ever use a knife unless I'm cutting up meat or something. The man tells me if I like the show. I tell him yeah, I watch it all the time at home. He tells me he used to watch this show with his kitty, but now his kitty was dead. I tell him, yeah, I know, Lino's outside with it, but, man, has he seen a pair of bolt cutters lying around here. Then I take another look down at the lady's snatch and she tells me there are days when she'd sell her soul for something good on TV, and what are bolt cutters. I tell them about the fat fuck having my bolt cutters somewhere around here and how I was needing them to do my job. Then the lady sucks on her bottle of beer and passes out like a baby. This whole fucked up show makes me want to adopt the fat fuck waiting for his stabbing downstairs. There the man was, crying and sucking on his bottle of beer, with the lady passed out with no panties. The fat fuck was having to look out for the lion and look out for himself. I'm still not looking at the man, so I keep my eyes on the snatch and tell him what they kill the lion for. What it ever do to them, and it was a good looking lion too.

The snatch moves and the lady opens her eyes. She tells me, nah-ah, what am I talking about kill. That was a suicide and the lion had mental problems. The man tells her to go fuck herself on account of she's the one always leaving the window open and the lion was too stupid not to throw itself out the window. The man tells me he misses his kitty and that maybe he should go outside and go bury it. I tell him, sure, man, whatever the fuck he wants. The man goes to put on some clothes over his boxers. I'm alone with the lady and she tells me that the lion was giving her Cancer with all the shit it left around and that she doesn't need Cancer in her house. I tell her, shit, lady, I get you, but does she mind if I look around the place for my bolt cutters. The lady just turns to click off my favorite TV show and I start searching for my bolt cutters.

I'm looking through a pile of clothes on the floor when the lady grabs onto my sleeve hard enough that I almost trip back. I tell her, lady, what's up. The lady's loaded up and fucked up and even though she looks me in the eyes and tells me hey, you want to fuck, let's fuck, the lion-killing snatch doesn't do it for me. I tell her I'm not interested, but if she could maybe later put on some pants or something and look for my bolt cutters that'd be real cool with me. She gets this hurt look on her and pouts up her lips and tells me that she was gonna tell me I was a cute looking kid with my flat, black hair. Just like Hitler's. She tells me she was gonna tell me I have Hitler hair but not anymore. I tell her don't sweat it and the man comes back wearing pants and t-shirt looking like a fucked up citizen and I head down to catch the family reunion with the man, the fat fuck and the lion. I don't find my bolt cutters but this shit is too good to miss.

The fat kid's just like I left him with his head petting the lion's brown spots. I tell him hey, man, your pops is here to bury this lion. He looks up and tells me the lion's gotten stiff. The man kneels down like he's meaning to touch the lion, but the fat fuck starts screaming for him to get away from him and his lion. The man smacks one across the fat fuck's face. The fat fuck still has the mark my Timberlands left matching his pop's handprint. I love this kind of shit, man. I love watching fights break out. So when the fat fuck's pops doesn't take off his belt or shoe or pick up something fucking sharp off the street I'm real bummed. The man gets up and tells the fat fuck it was his cat not the fat fuck's and he's gonna take it and bury it, so he'd better back up and let him at that lion. The fat fuck's still holding on to the lion and the man has to smack him one more after all. I'm standing back and laughing wishing I had popcorn and one last smack gets the man his lion.

The man lifts the lion on his shoulder, and it's the weirdest fucking thing walking a stiff lion with its paws sticking out like Superman flying and its tail pointing straight out like a dick.

I tell the fat fuck not to worry on account of maybe his pops would buy him a new lion. The fat fuck turns into a mute and it's the saddest fucking funeral march you'd ever want to see.

It's the three of us by ourselves on this train heading to Fort Tyron Park to bury the lion, not counting this homeless dude who comes up to us and asks to pet the lion. I tell him, hey, man, you're drunk. He tells me yeah, and that it's real easy to get drunk after you give blood. I tell him he's not fucking petting any lion and I'd smack him one with my Timberlands but I don't want to get that homeless smell on them. The homeless dude backs away telling me he ain't never seen a lion before. Meanwhile, the fat fuck and his pops are stoned into like a grief, man, staring at the windows and thinking thoughts, and I'm feeling I should be wearing black. I tell the man, we need shovels, man. To dig the earth. My voice comes out all soft on account of respect for the dead lion. Nah, the man tells me. We're gonna use our hands. Then the man tells me the lion was put blind when the lady poured rubbing alcohol into its eyes. I tell him, that's fucked up, what the lady do that for. The man shrugs and starts petting his head on the lion's brown spots just like the fat fuck only way skinnier.

Better than watching the fat fuck get his head smacked in by his pops is watching the fat fuck beat on the man with my bolt cutters. The fat fuck had 'em down his pants the whole time and I'm getting that I've just been betrayed and this fat fuck was gonna keep my property and steal his own bikes with 'em and leave me out in the cold with no money for new Timberlands and shit. I try to cut short the man's beating so I can get my bolt cutters but the fat fuck bites my arm. I scream out and I hear the homeless dude laughing. The fat fuck's acting like a lion, sitting on top of the man, with blood all on his clothes and blood coming out of the man's head and the blood oozing all on the train floor and blood spots on the subway map behind me. My arm stings like a bitch and I lift my Timberlands up on my seat and the fat fuck's finally had enough beating that he sits down with his man boobs breathing heavy. He sits across from me and I'm not even trying to get revenge on my arm when he's still got my bolt cutters. He tells me they killed Arthur. I tell him who the fuck's Arthur. He beats the seat next to him one with the bolt cutters and tells me I'm a dumb fuck. Arthur's his lion. I don't tell the fat fuck that Arthur's a pussy name for a lion. I point down to the man and tell the fat fuck something big just happened, this is a real thing he's got. The homeless dude inches his way up to the lion that fell under the seats when the fat fuck jumped on the man. The train doors open with a ding-ding and what else could I do: I tell the fat fuck the homeless dude is trying to steal his lion, then I tell him Adios. Then I jump over the puddle of blood in front of me and shoot myself out the train doors right before they close real Indian Jones style, ya know. I leave the fat fuck, I leave the man, I leave the homeless dude and I leave the lion behind, I'm up the steps, I'm through the turnstile, I wink at the black chick in the booth, I'm outside, it's morning.

I didn't ever see the fat kid after he busted up the man and went to jail, but I heard about him all over. This one guy said that Lino'd been raising a baby dolphin in his tub. But that was bullshit I told the guy because I'd been to Lino's and all I'd seen was the man and the lady. I even saw the lady over by Riverside the other day. She didn't look like she was missing the man or her boy. She saw me and blew me a kiss. I walked off the other way cuz I wasn't looking for another dead lion.

Mademoiselle

Jean Richepin *(translated by J. Boyett)*

He was listed at the town hall as Jean-Marie-Mathieu Valot; but everyone called him Mademoiselle.

He was the village idiot.

But not one of those pathetic idiots in rags, who live off public charity. He lived quite well, from a small income left him by his mother, and honestly administered by his guardian. Thus he inspired more envy than pity.

Nor was he one of those menacing idiots, half animal, who disgust or horrify. He was a joy to see, with his forever-parted lips and his forever-smiling eyes, and especially with the perpetual masquerade of his feminine accoutrements.

For he dressed as a girl, thus showing how far from disagreeable to him was the nickname, "Mademoiselle."

And how could he not have loved it, this name uttered by his mother like a sweet caress back when he was a babe, so delicate, so feeble, his complexion frail and sickly, a poor little unfinished boy, less energetic than many girls his age? It was as an affectionate caress that his mother, from his first years, had whispered to him this tender "Mademoiselle," while his old grandmother gaily repeated, "By my faith, it's not worth a Christian's trouble to even talk about what he's got for a weenie, may the good lord forgive me saying so."

And the grandfather, no less gay, would usually add, "Let's just hope it doesn't fall off as he grows, like a tadpole tail!"

And they treated him like a real girl, doting on him, all the more so since the household was doing well and didn't need a male to raise it up in the world.

Once the grandparents and the mother were dead, Mademoiselle was hardly less happy with his paternal uncle, a doctor who'd stayed a bachelor, and cared for the idiot as best he could, growing more and more attached as he did so. With this gentleman, as well, Jean-Marie-Mathieu Valot continued to be called Mademoiselle.

The whole countryside called him that, never with any hurtful intention, but on the contrary with each person wanting only to give pleasure to the poor gentle soul who had never harmed anyone.

Not even the children meant any malice by it, accustomed as they were to greeting the great innocent when he went out in his dress and bonnet. What would have struck them as extraordinary, and would have pushed them to some mischief, would have been seeing him dressed as a boy.

But Mademoiselle was far from doing that. Like his nickname, his clothes were dear to him. He delighted in wearing them and in nothing else, with the particular refinement that he knew perfectly well he was not a girl and was living in a disguise.

One could see that by the exaggeratedly feminine affectation he adopted, as if to show that this affectation was not natural to him. His enormous bonnet, meticulously frilled, sheltered monstrous, multicolored garnitures of ribbons. His skirt splayed out in numerous pleats, ballooning out behind, reinforced by great hoops. He walked with tiny little steps, with extravagant twists and hip-sways, his arms pulled in against his chest and his hands fanned out and wagging in pretentious, comically coquettish gestures.

To be his friend, one had to say seriously to him, "Oh, Mademoiselle! How good you are at being a girl!"

That would put him in a good mood, and he would joyfully reply, "Aren't I? But you can see it's only for a laugh."

Nevertheless, at the countryside celebrations, when they danced in the town square, he wanted to be invited as "Mademoiselle," and never invited a girl himself.

One evening, someone having asked him why not, he opened his eyes wide, laughed as if at something stupid, and said, "But I don't want to invite any girls, since I'm not dressed as a boy. Look at my dress, imbecile!"

Being a sensible man, his questioner retorted, "Dress as a boy, then, Mademoiselle."

He reflected an instant; then, with a sneaky air, said, "But if I dress as a boy, I'll no longer be Mademoiselle. And since I *am* Mademoiselle!..."

And he shrugged his shoulders.

Still, he must have dwelled on the notion. For, upon encountering the sensible man sometime later, he said to him brusquely, "If I dress as a boy, will you still call me Mademoiselle?"

"Of course," replied the other. "You'll always be called that."

The idiot seemed enchanted. No doubt, he valued his nickname even more than his costume. The next day, he was seen arriving on the square free of his skirts and dressed as a man. He had taken pants, a riding coat and a hat from his guardian's wardrobe.

This was a revolution for the town.

The people, who were accustomed to giving him friendly smiles when he was dressed in women's clothes, stared at him with alarm, with an astonished and hostile-seeming air. The most indulgent couldn't help but laugh, with clear mockery.

The involuntary hostility of some, the too-apparent mockery of others, the disagreeable stupefaction of all these people shaken out of an old habit: the idiot fully perceived it all and suffered from it.

It was worse still, when the first child started singing out, as he pranced around him, "Hey! Mademoiselle's got pants! Hey, Mademoiselle!"

And it grew more and more frightful as a whole band of hoodlums followed at his heels, hollering, jeering, like they were after a town drunk.

Now, much more than before, the unfortunate boy appeared disguised. In having lived as a girl, and always exaggerating his feminine airs, he had completely lost all boyish physiognomy. His smooth face, his long flaxen hair, all cried out for the beribboned bonnet and became a caricature under the tall top hat of the old doctor. In the fatherly riding coat, in the too-large shorts, Mademoiselle's chest and especially his bouncing backside danced wildly. And nothing was funnier than the contrast between this grave attire and the tiny-trotting pace, the precious carriage of the head, the pretentious gesture of hands fanned out like a little girl's.

Soon the youths, the old gossips, even the mature men and, notably, the sensible counselor, all joined with the urchins to jeer at Mademoiselle.

The stunned idiot took off running and returned home terrified.

There, he held his poor head in both hands and tried to comprehend. Why did they resent him? For they did resent him, clearly. What had he done wrong, who had he hurt, in dressing like a boy? Wasn't he a boy, after all?

And, for the first time in his life, he felt horror at his nickname. Wasn't it with that nickname that they'd insulted him?

Then a horrible suspicion came to him: "If I were a mademoiselle for real?..."

He would have liked to consult his guardian, but didn't dare. Besides, he had a vague idea that the good man might not tell him the truth, out of complacency. And he preferred to work it out by himself, rather than ask anything of anyone.

All his idiot's cunning, till then latent because he'd never had an occasion to use it, now blossomed and pushed him towards a dark and solitary action.

He once again dressed as a girl the next day and reappeared with an air of having perfectly forgotten his escapade of the day before.

The people, and especially the children, had not forgotten it at all. They looked at him sideways, not even the best among them hid their ironic smiles. The children went back to following him and shouting, "Hey! Mademoiselle had some pants!"

But he acted like he didn't understand, like he didn't even suspect what they were alluding to. As before, he showed himself gay, a joy to look at, lips always parted and eyes always smiling. As before, he sported enormous, multicolored bonnets, billowing skirts. As before, he walked with mincing steps, swayed at the hips, twisted at the waist, made coquettish gestures, and licked his lips with a sensual tongue whenever someone called him "Mademoiselle," even though deep down he now wanted to leap at their throats.

Days, months passed, and finally those around him no longer remembered the strange escapade which seemed to be so profoundly abolished from his memory.

But he never ceased to think of it, nor to keep watch, perpetually on tenterhooks, for a chance to learn how he would recognize his boy's nature and how he would victoriously prove it. A true innocent, he had reached the age of twenty without learning what that nature consisted of, without ever even having been moved to try to find out.

Tenacious and curious and deceitful, he never asked any questions, and he observed. Often, during dances, he heard the boys brag about girls they'd turned bad, the girls boast about such or such boy. And often, after the ball, he watched interlaced couples leave. People barely paid attention to him. He listened. He spied.

At last, he saw the thing plain and simple, several times (for he wanted to be absolutely sure); he had the joy of knowledge.

And one night, as the dances had just ended and couples were leaving, holding each other by the waist, a loud cry came from the corner of the woods one went through to reach the neighboring village. It was Joséphine, the beautiful Joséphine, calling for help. A good girl, who was going home alone, for she was a brave girl as well. They ran to her call.

They arrived to tear her, gasping, from the grip of Mademoiselle who was raping her, having strangled her already.

The idiot had watched her, had jumped on her to do what the other boys did to girls. She had resisted valiantly. So he had wrapped his hands around her neck and squeezed with all his strength. She had passed out. She was dying. And quickly, quickly, he was rushing to prove to himself that he was a boy.

In freeing Joséphine, they had roughly thrown him to the ground, half knocking him out. Now all of a sudden here he was, jumping up, foaming, drooling, crying out:

"I'm not a mademoiselle anymore. I'm a boy, I'm a boy, I tell you!"

And, skirts hiked up, he proudly shook in the moonlight a poor, flaccid, trembling little piece of macaroni.

Three Dogs

by Jon Rachmani

I.

I turned around, from the waist up, I should say, moving that part of my frame that gave easy way while keeping my feet in place. And again I made this motion. And it was the same as before. Each time it was the same as before. Each time I turned and each time he was there, following me. The Detective, I thought, by which I mean to say this is the name I applied to him in the privacy of my silence, because he always followed me. And each time I tried running off to escape him he'd be back in a few hours, next time I went out, the next day, as soon as I turned the corner and went out into the sunlight, in a word, inevitably.

I turned the corner and tried to catch my breath. My breath had been more and more haggard. I, my body, also haggard, worn, drawn, by what those who saw me and chose to comment in my presence reported to me in those days.

And in those days he followed me when I went out for lunch, or rather when I went out searching, my stomach sour with a hunger in which there stood no conviction. "I'm so hungry," I would say, "that if I was following him instead of the situation as it is, which I am loath to describe lest I plummet, I would speed up, get right up behind him and swallow him down, swallow him down to his toes and get it over with."

And this time I decided to get the whole thing over with, and by thing I mean affair, and after the third time I turned around I made to sprint off like usual and took a couple sylphish leaps, but then stopped in my leaps and I turned a fourth time. He was standing still, some several paces behind me. And he must have bolted too, bolted after me as I bolted, and bolted faster than my bolt, for he was closer than he'd even been before and I could look at his features now.

Now, his features were upsetting to me. I looked at them and I saw that the dark blue and dark green that faded out around his eyes made him look like he'd been beaten about the face or was starving even more than I. Starving more than I! And what made his features upsetting to me was more the balls themselves, the enormous, oblong eyeballs, than the darkness that ringed them, about which I commented just previously. But eyes, eyes, the eyes. Cow eyes, yes, in size, but more than that, misshapen eyes that I can't remember having seen blink in all the time that I looked at them at that moment of examination, which was considerable indeed.

It took considerable effort to do what next I did do. I said, loud, for him to hear, "You're closer than you've ever been before. Your features are upsetting to me. You stand ten paces away from me. You see me through blinkless cowballeyes ringed in dark stains." After I was finished with my words I didn't close my mouth, because I never close my mouth, and when I saw him say nothing I said again, "You're closer than you've ever been before. Your features are upsetting to me. You stand ten paces away from me. And you know how you see me—I've told you already—but even if I hadn't you still would know, because it is your position to use them and it is mine, it is my position, forever it seems, does it not? considering your propensities, to have them used against me." I admit that I discerned a slight disquiet in my own words. And again I left my mouth open after my words but this time I was soon clapped with a new matter that cut the other short and slipped shut my lips.

He spoke.

He spoke, and still we stood there on the bending avenue, ladies in shawls passing by with children, delivery men under the burden of bulging packages, dogs trotting by, either in groups or as solo padders of the urban flatness, with frogs or chew sticks propping open their ample jaws. A fat woman in a motorized wheelchair passed by me smoking a cigar, the wheel of her chair passing close by my toes where they lay concealed under the makings of my shoe. But more than the moving elements of the scene that come into my remembering mind like milk from large breast to small mouth, was the abundance of enormous taverns on the street, each offering selections of variously cooked meats at prices ranging from motley pittances to enormous askings.

Yes he spoke. And though it was but a pittance of words, they were for me. And with his words I approached. That is, as he spoke I moved my body, feet and all this time closer to him.

It was, "I don't care," that he said. And soon after he was done I was what must have been within only many inches of him. I thought I saw his eyes bulge, and I stiffened my legs so they wouldn't run off.

It was, "You feel guilty, don't you? But it doesn't stop you from coming back," that I said in return. Get to the point, this, since the beginning of my awareness of my own manner, has always been a policy of mine to which I have, in best faith, adhered.

No words came from his mouth, and no more came from mine either, but first my stomach churned and boomed, and, following mine, his adhered to the same deep tones. I let my eyes flit up near to looking at his again, though I dared not let them go all the way, and a pang not worth description in this chronicle—excluded merely for purposes of the maintenance of concision—rose up and mingled with that of my hunger. I turned away my head and with it my eyes and looked up and down the street for a place to, if you will, eat.

We walked, beside one another, like a bright thing and a dark thing, the one the copy of the other, and it was in this fashion that we were because the sun that shone on me, revealing every detail, was blocked from falling on him by the very fact of what I have just stated, though parenthetically.

But you must allow a brief digression before the action in earnest gets under way: though we walked, brisk, from one storefront to another, once we cupped our faces up to the glass, such was the intensity of what I took to be the sunshine as to merit such extremities, we were faced, more times that I care here to impart upon your no doubt well-attending minds without needlessly pummeling you with irrelevancies, with meat shops at which every table stood ringed with eaters, leaving no proper room for myself and my Detective.

At one establishment the owner, I presume, his fed stomach distended over a wide leather belt, came outside and, addressing us in sober tones, thumbed back at his meat shop. "How many more can I fit in that room?" he said.

Wanting now satiation more than accustomed elegance, I closed my eyes to the large man and spoke the truth: "I'm going to die. Now I need to eat or I will kill you."

"You'll kill me." This was his surprised and, I would hesitate not to add, angry riposte.

"I need your help," I riposted in a change of tactics that caused an anticipatory rumble to cross from my Detective's stomach to mine, as though some reality of his imparted itself on me, or perhaps I'm getting it backwards.

And a meat server, or what I took to be one, had joined us outside the establishment. Judging from his proportionally large arms I suspected to assist in a possible removal of persons. But the owner, or the man I presumed to fit that style, merely tousled his greased locks and said, "Put those two inside and close the door." The owner then removed cigarettes in package from his pocket and turned from us.

The meat server then opened the door and pushed us through together, and my Detective and I were within whiff of food.

"And again. And again. And again," the maitre'd insisted on seeing us.

And I pointed to the two men outside and exclaimed the permission that accompanied us on our ingress, and she, this maitre'd, turned from me, her sharp hips showing through her dress, and I for a moment had to restrain myself by pushing in on my air-filled paunch just to keep myself from impaling my foul physique on the edge of that bone. But soon she had turned from us into the crowd.

Speaking into the crowd, "I can't stand it," I said.

"Stop it. How can you say that?" said the Detective. And I, through my open mouth, smiled at him for the first time, letting my eyes blur over in the act so I wouldn't have to smile and see his cowballs in their width at the same moment lest it end me. And together, more so than ever before, I admit with mist, we pushed our way hard past a rippled candle of a woman and her bony, dying children, children pallid as though kept locked in a back room, who blocked the path to the meat.

A scream from the maitre'd, "Go back." She waved the blades of her hands. But, together, a crashing wave, complete with rumble, we pushed through, authorized, synchronized, starving, and in love.

The blade of his shoulder bone crunching like parched earth beneath my shod toes, one of the starvelings wailed out, "Mommy."

On this parched earth nothing is achieved without the death of an innocent. Partial and contributory evidence? our successful glide through the pressed flesh that smelled like a toilet activity that, fortunately for those of us with good taste, has yet to be named to my knowledge, to a lopsided table at the back. There we stood, mangled together. It would have been hard to delineate between his limbs and mine, such was our tortured proximity. And until our portions arrived we went in silence, taking in the sneers from those others at the table whom we'd crowded and avoiding their cross board salivations. But once the meat came I began to question my Detective with mouth full of red flesh.

My mouth full of red flesh, I said, "You keep coming back because you're trying to kill me."

And then, sibling of mine—may I so denominate you?—he came out with a line that made all the meat I'd already swallowed pour out from between my drenched lips, pour out already chewed and acidified, mixed with mucus and flecked with pinpoints of my own blood, he said, and still smiling may I add without causing dullness in your imagination as it follows this account, "I keep coming back because I'm not cured yet."

My throat sour, my mouth a veritable sewer, I wailed, timed, I might add, with a crash of my fists against the table that provoked a crash of fists against my person on the part of the two armed slaves standing on the side of my body not inhabited by this most brutal of detectives, "How long are you going to keep coming back?"

I kept my mouth wide and let my Detective see the hollow that passed through me. Though it reeked, I brought the mouth level with his horrible eyes in the most brutal way, as though I'd print there some further fetid expulsion, and he said, still cool, "Your lips are enormous, you're the Healer. You're the Healer, aren't you?"

"Stop," I yelled, even through the pain of what was now a litany of punches and pinches from all corners save the Detective's.

"Stop," he also, but was too late to save.

I.

I should start from the beginning. For months before I went to the doctor there had been a pain inside my chest that crept between the heart and the lungs. It would wake me in the first minutes of dawn and I'd jerk up to sitting in my dirty bed and I would stare from the window at the pale early light. Was that the sun? I'd wonder.

But the doctor was no help—after an examination with his soap-smelling, cool hands he told me that there was little he could do and began writing a prescription for a drug he said would make most of the pain go away. He said I would have to stay in my bed and I thought about the unclean thing, the place of early awakening, its sheets unwashed, and about the white worms I found sometimes in my blanket. I begged him to cure me, to not give me the drug, to bring me back to health instead. He shook his head at me, but stopped writing the prescription.

Then he asked me if I had yet been to The Healer and I said that I had not. "Who was The Healer?" I asked.

"She lives in the apartment upstairs, above my office. She sees men like yourself, who need to be cured."

"And does she cure them?"

"So far as I can understand, she does. But I'm only a doctor, you know."

I left his office and looked back through the crack of the door. He sat behind his desk, his head cocked, with a wince in his eyes. His poised pen was still in his hand. For a moment I thought it had turned into a knife, but I was wrong, it was still a pen.

"Are you going to close the door?" he said.

I opened it a little more till the light was in both my eyes. "I don't know," I said. "Do you prefer it closed?"

"I'd like it if you could decide for yourself. I'm too busy right now."

I waited for him to move his head.

"What are you waiting for?" he said.

"I thought you would move."

"I have work."

I shut the door, my gaze on him till the end, and made sure it fit into the frame without much noise.

The doctor's office was on the second floor so I thought that the Healer's would be on the third, but I didn't get my hopes up. Where the staircase to the second floor was lit by three bulbs, the staircase further up, going to what I hoped would be the third floor, had no bulbs, and only dim light from below helped me not to fall to my death. And a hand on the wall.

Up on the landing it was darker. I let my fingers brush against the concrete of the wall until they reached a seam and then a wooden panel.

I knocked on it.

"No!" came a scream from the other side. It was a woman's voice.

The Healer, I thought.

I knocked again, harder. "No! Stop it." The sound of her voice made me laugh. I should keep knocking, I thought. I banged again and again, with increasing strength. The wood was thin and the sensation of it bending against my knuckles was pleasurable. "No! No! No! Not again, not today, not ever—go slit your throat and let the dogs have you. I'm finished." I laughed more and kept banging, but then pulled away my arm and pressed both my hands to the left side of my chest. It was the pain again. It opened up and throbbed with an inhale. I kept my breaths shallow and pressed down till the pain was lesser.

I reached down and found the doorknob. I tried it. The door was locked. I shook the knob.

"Stop! You'll kill me if you don't stop."

I banged my fist again and said, as loud as I could manage in what was sudden embarrassment at speaking through a door, "I need to see the Healer, or I'll die. If you leave me out here you'll kill me."

There was no more response from the other side. I thought it was getting colder in the hallway, but with so little light I couldn't be sure. My senses weren't strong and I didn't know what color my hands were. But I thought it was colder and I was scared now to knock again.

I waited a long time and breathed, and the cold air in my chest made the pain sharper.

The door opened. The light coming through was intense to my eyes.

I vomited. From the light. And the pain. It was thin and acrid against my tongue, and the taste was so bad that with each gulp I sickened myself further and heaved harder. In between waves I looked up. Her silhouette. Each time I looked up it was closer. The wide hips, the narrow chest, the diffuse light through the unkempt hair.

"Stop!" she yelled and slapped me on the back. To stop the gagging, I guess. It worked.

I lifted my hands, which were grasping my bent knees, and I let my weight fall to the left and got around her and took myself as fast as I could toward the open door.

"Stop!" she still yelled. But I was inside, my eyes closed against the light coming in through the windows. Was that the sun?

I heard the door shut and I turned around and forced my face into a squint so I'd see what was happening. I looked at her. "You're the Healer, aren't you?" I said.

"How dare you?" she asked. I opened my eyes further. I liked looking at her. Her eyes, small, pink, were rimmed with dark blue and green. The skin on her face shone in the light, looked wet, and her lips were huge. They were so big and looked so heavy on her thin face that I was riveted and I didn't know what to do not to look at them.

"Your lips are enormous," I said. She didn't move. There was the sound of giggles from the side and I looked for a minute at an interior door to that side. I looked back at her. "You're the Healer."

She put her hands on the sides of her head, flat. "How long are you going to keep coming back?"

I was furious. "I keep coming back," I said, and started walking toward her, slow as I could, "because I'm not cured yet."

"You keep coming back because you're trying to kill me," she whispered, and her lips shook.

The interior door opened. I stopped approaching her and turned to see what it was doing.

A little boy with kinky red hair and light brown skin had opened it and stood there, his hand still on the knob. "Mommy," he said. He licked his lips. He frowned. His eyes were almost as big as her lips.

"Go back," I said.

"Stop it!" she said to me. "How can you say that?" She walked to him, her hips even ampler in the light, their blades well padded. I could open my eyes to it all the way now. She picked him up. She kissed his face. Her lips went flat against his cheek and his hands went to her breasts.

I looked down. I pressed a hand against my chest. I wanted to kill them both but I knew I didn't have the strength, so I waited. But just to bang them against each other and use each one to bash the other one in. Did I smile then?

But then from behind the door again. A baby crawling. Crying out of its foreign eyes, the lids folded over and down.

"I can't stand it," I said.

She put the boy back on his feet, picked up the crying infant, and opened the door wide. "And again, and again," she said. "And again."

It was a small room with not so much light, full of children. I took a few steps forward just to see. Some were infants like the second that had come out. Some naked and some with rags around their genitals. Some were older, like the first one, and wore pajamas or dirtied nightshirts. And a few were probably past thirteen. Yes, there was that one who sat in the stool on the corner, the girl with the blonde hair, who held one of the small ones and stared at me the whole time the door was open. She was in rags and had lips almost as thick as her mother's. And all of them of different colors and features, except that some, like the girl in the chair, shared features with the Healer.

"Put those two inside and close the door," I said.

She did. She put them in and closed the door. Did she know I would have hurt them? I heard a baby's cry through the wall once she'd done it. "I need your help," I said.

"You'll kill me," she said. She stared at me a long time, the dark around the pink shrinking down on it.

"I'm going to die," I told her. "Now I need to be healed or I will kill you." I was furious.

"You feel guilty, don't you?" she said. "But it doesn't stop you from coming back. How many more can I fit in that room?"

"I don't care," I said.

"Unbutton my dress." I went behind her and squeezed the oblong buttons through their ragged holes and then pushed the dress off her shoulders. "Now burn me down," she said, "burn me down to a nub and get it over with. But it won't work any better this time."

And, for all my disgust, I did. What else was I to do?

I.

I was still hung over from the night before, but I went to the party anyway, because I knew he'd be there and I'd promised myself to confront him weeks before. The anticipation had begun to make me lose sleep.

I was late. The first of the guests, a couple whom I knew slightly, passed through the apartment house's lobby just when I went in.

"Hey," one said and patted my arm.

"How was it? Is he still there?"

I didn't have to ask if they knew whom I meant. They thought of us as great friends.

"Oh he's there all right. He's smashed. See you." And they were gone.

I climbed the steps into the lobby and felt it press against my leg. Warmed by my anticipation, it felt like a rigid finger pressing into my thigh. Why had I brought it? I couldn't understand. I'd never done anything like that before. It was not the first time I had felt myself betrayed by a friend, it was not even a particularly stunning betrayal, so why the knife? But I touched it through the fabric with my fingertips and in the elevator looked down to see if it made a visible bulge. It did. But not enough for anyone to take notice. Besides, it could have been anything making that bulge.

The apartment's door was a crack ajar. It was the sort of party where the door was left open, where the guests were meant to come and go unannounced, where all you did to leave was whisper something in the host's ear long enough to make her laugh and then make smiling eye contact with those you'd spoken to, because the same people and the same banter would pick up again at someone else's place within the week anyway.

In the foyer I let my right hand slide into my pants' pocket. Not on the side with the bulge. I was surprised. There was a tissue in there that had gone through the wash, smooth and hard like a lightweight pebble. I took it out and looked at it, there in that elegant foyer where the twenty or so voices of happy party-goers clattered in my ears like cutlery against cutlery. On the hall table sat a big antique magnifying glass, some antique puzzle boxes, and a bowl of house keys. And you can imagine, in such camera-ready prettiness, the strangeness of that ovoid tissue rolling between my fingers. But stranger still is what I did next. Without thinking, I squeezed the tissue and cracked it open, revealed the hidden folds of the paper itself, lifted it to my face, printed there the expulsion of my nostrils, and let it fall to the floor, where it sat, white and yellow and nearly aglow, beside a neat stack of oversized magazines. I looked down at the front of my pants again and went into the party to let myself be known.

The first place my eyes went in the crowded room was to a corner in which Tom and Bradford were talking. They stood, each tilted three quarters toward the wall, their voices dampened, controlled, but still too loud to hold their argumentative tone. How odd, I thought. A fight! I had known all these people so long and no one had fought in years. Who fought anymore, anyway? Who had the stamina? Sure, couples' tiffs and blowups, but even those were usually postponed till after hours. Tom raised his hand, flat and sharp, and it quivered in front of Bradford's face. "Well, that's not what he told me, someone's lying, someone's GUILTY for—" something, he said.

I walked, so far unnoticed, to the back wall where stood the smoked glass and ebony bar and reached under the counter for a stem. My eyes fixed for that moment on the framed and signed photograph of a dog on the street lapping at a textured pool that in the black and white shot remained ambiguous, that hung above the bottles. That was me up there. I poured myself a glass of claret, drank it, poured myself another, drank it, and then, careful not to be noticed stealing the most expensive substance in the house, filled a snifter from the small bottle on the top shelf above the photograph.

I then went out to a group where a woman I didn't know stood talking to Jack and Valencia. I passed the required minute of passive listening with my nose buried in the snifter.

"It was this Nepalese yak's milk cheese, very pungent, with foie gras and pan grille, and it was really, really good, especially with that wine," Valencia said. My eyes met hers for a moment. I took my nose out of the glass and gave her and then Jack my usual frown. Jack knew that she and I had lost control a few times, but that had been last season. I stared for a second at the woman I didn't know, who, even with three-inch heels, only came up to my shoulder, a stub of a woman, and hoped she wouldn't ask me my name.

They talked about food a little more, and then about football, and then about a certain commercial that coincided with the football, and then about a suburban girl whose face was often broadcast who had been abducted that spring and had been found the day before by some spelunkers in a deep cave near the northern border. She was alive, though her sense organs had been mutilated, and she was set to do the talk show circuit.

"Has he," I said at a natural pause and gestured with my glass toward my friend, where he sat on the edge of the sofa, surrounded by lip-licking auditors, the host's kitten in his lap, "has he been talking a whole lot this evening? You know?"

"Excuse us a moment," Jack said, and Valencia just walked into the kitchen with Jack behind her.

"Drink this!" someone yelled from the kitchen once they had disappeared.

The short woman said something.

"Did you ask me my name?" I said, and encased my nose again.

"No, I just asked what just happened."

"Oh," I said and took a little sip, "that was what we, my friend, if I may deign to call you that, would call the rebuff."

She laughed. I don't know why. "Yeah, I know that, but give me the gossip, what's going on?"

"You're a little drunk." She laughed again and nodded. "Do you know the man I pointed to?"

"No. I work with Jack, he and Val just dragged me out, I don't know anyone here."

"Well then," I said, relishing my position, "I'll tell you the story of me and my friend over there. His name is Jon. We've known each other since boarding school, where we were roommates. Even right now, when I look at him, I still see that lanky sixteen-year-old who never took off his tie till he went to bed, who paced the boards of our room reading to me from the Hermetics. I've never been one for reading, especially not anything foggy—those horrible books where you do your best to follow the argument, finish the first chapter confident, lean back in bed for a smoke, pick up again in chapter two and you feel like you're reading the first chapter of an unrelated book, with arguments twice as hard to trace. He recited to spite me."

"And all this time you've stayed friends?" the little woman, who seemed to have grown an inch or so, like a candle burning in reverse, said, something of real interest in her pleated brow.

"Yes. All this time. Right up to this very moment we have been the best of friends. And this is where the secret lies, where the hidden bond no one knows about is to be found. But ... I'll let you in on the secret, just a little bit." She shook her head, but I knew she couldn't wait for me to go on. "I trust you. You look ... private. I'd like to hear what you think of this. The secret, you see, is that back then in boarding school, after I'd sneak back into our room from a party on another floor or from visiting a girl in town, drunk or high or physically spent, you understand, I'd flop onto my bed and pass out. But not always pass out. And I knew what he'd do then. He'd come over to my bed after a little wait, sit on the side, and say, 'You awake?' Then louder, 'You awake?' And once he'd satisfied himself that I was insensible, I'd soon feel the heat of his hand on my shoulder. 'You awake?' And when I still said nothing the hand would go to my stomach and the question would sound again. Then to my leg. 'I'm just going to have to play Detective for a second, I hope you understand, I just want to make sure you're okay,' he'd say, and undo the zipper of my trousers. And he'd manipulate me in this way I don't know how often—I really don't. Feeling around for the straight thing and the ovate things down there. He delights, you see, in handling people like us. But me—was it shame that kept me from revealing what I knew? Was it some secret desire for it to go on? These are the questions at hand. And you understand, he still does it to me." She gave me wide eyes. "Metaphorically. The one thing this sort of people will teach you is just how useful metaphors can be. And it's a metaphor that I'm using when I cite his continued and sustained abuse. But let me tell you how tied we've been, how entwined we've become—"

I was cut off by a sudden silence in the room. And then, "Ladies and gentleman," Jon said and stood, the kitten raised in his left hand, "I don't know why I'm still holding this adorable beast, but it helps you to make your case if you've got something cute up your sleeve." Everyone laughed. What else could they have done? This is what he did, always, this is how he crushed people. This is what I'm trying to get you to see. "Ladies and gentlemen, it has come to my inebriated attention that my very close friend is ..." his eyes rolled and he nearly dropped the kitten. A general gasp. And even this—do you see? "That he is pointedly ignoring me." Suzie scoffed, the host grinned, the guy with those glasses that went dark under the sun and always stayed a little dim turned a backward slump in his chair into a forward one. Everyone was anxious, of course, to hear what was coming next. "Cameron, if you don't mind, could you flick off the TV a moment?" Cameron, who sat by the set, turned off the shock cinema film that was playing, right in the middle of a sadistic sex scene. "Thank you—good man." Jon lifted the kitten to his lips, kissed it, and put it down to scamper away. But it just sat at his feet and purred, rubbed the side of its head against his cuff. "I was saying, my dear friends, that one in our company has been ignoring me and I think we all know why, and that is my fault, my indiscretion." My blood pounded throughout me so hard that it felt like the knife itself was throbbing against my leg. "And so since I'm the one to have made what for most stays private so very public over the years, and since it has at last come back to my friend himself, I wish to tell you all the story of our friendship so that maybe you'll understand better, and so that maybe his so very delicate pride might at last be spared." Without daring to look in anyone's eyes, I gulped back the rest of the golden fluid in the snifter and moved away from the short woman, to the bar, where I propped myself so I wouldn't fall. "The two of us have been in a less than harmonious dance since we first met at Anastasia's garden party last year, and for this part we are, both of us, culpable. He had only recently moved to the city and knew only a few people. I took it upon myself that night to guide him, make introductions. Because I just enjoy that sort of thing, whoever it's for. The problem was, though, and this I blame him for entirely, that he couldn't stop telling lies, embarrassing me by making false claims to an intimacy with me that simply never existed, doing this for his own advantage—even to this day he lies to everyone he meets. And he does it because he has nothing else to say, because he's too weak to stand up without me, to stand up tall and stiff on his own and so he uses poor me as a prop, and my only sin in the matter has been to repeat of late the stories of his I've heard from one person to someone with a contradictory account, as though the stories were about different people entirely, with no sense to be made of them. A great deal of resentment has come down on him for that, of course, and for that," he said, flashing his eyes at mine, "I am sorry. But I—I here and now ABSOLVE myself—"

It was there that he broke off with a gasp. Between us, between me and my long-lost friend, there was only one point of common contact, and it shone bright in the candlelight. Our friends were backed up against the furniture, no one was going to intervene. It was time for me to leave. I passed through the foyer, saw my tissue still on the floor by the oversized magazines where I'd dropped it, and left the party, my pockets empty, my mind at rest.

Plastic Factory

Ron Kolm

I.

My name is Ron, I work in a plastics factory. The particular factory I work in is new, and it squats atop a man-made mound of grass-covered rubble. In front of it is a large asphalt parking lot with an access road tying it to a major highway which, in turn, eventually bypasses a medium-sized city. To one side of the factory are miles of flat sparse fields, traveling out to a low range of blue mountains in the distance. The other side drops down to a curve in the expressway.

The factory itself is modern architecture at its most functional and banal; the one-storied rectangular box. Only three appendages break this stark harmony; a loading dock on the left front, the main door on the right front (giving the design balance), and a toolshed in back. Halfway down the steep embankment, between the factory and the highway, is a small square concrete structure. We call it the "pillbox."

The factory's interior is split along its length into two equal halves by a spacious hallway. Access to this hall is controlled by the office, the first cubicle on the right side. The main entrance leads into this office. Continuing down the hall, we pass on our right the locker room, where the employees change into their white smocks, the bathrooms and the dispensary, and finally a modern, well-lit cafeteria, with its plastic chairs and formica'd tables, and its banks of tall bright fast-food machines. If we retrace our steps back to the front of the building, and list the rooms on our left as we repeat our journey towards the rear, we first pass an immense space directly behind the loading dock. This is the inspection, packing and shipping room. Beyond this, protected by thick double walls of cinderblock, is the pressure cooking room, the room I work in. My shift runs from three o'clock in the afternoon to midnight, with an hour break for lunch, which is really dinner. There is only one other person who works this shift with me, and the reason for this is the brand-newness of our plant.

Over fifty people work in this factory during the first shift, which starts at six in the morning and ends at three. (First shift sets their alarm clocks for five A.M. They awake in pitch darkness.) Second shift (my shift) is being built up gradually. There is no third shift. (The factory is closed between twelve and six.) So far, just the two of us.

Most of the employees have what they consider to be decent jobs. They wear clean smocks. They work in a clean, safe area. They're allowed to listen to portable radios. And they get paid fairly well, all things considered equal. But for my partner and me, and for our counterparts on the first shift, conditions are somewhat different.

You see, what the inspectors are inspecting, and the packers are packing, and the shippers shipping, what the people in the office are drawing up bills and invoices for, what the investors are making money on, are lenses for eye-glasses, but not ordinary glass lenses, no. The lenses we manufacture are made of plastic, using a new and still-secret process. This secret is guarded in many and ingenious ways; for instance the entire building, and the pillbox outside, are wired to Wells Fargo, and so on.

But let us discuss the process, itself. A mixture containing styrene (an oil-based fluid) and an exmer, is poured (or inserted) into a form, which is placed in a giant pressure-cooker, and baked (or broiled, or what have you). The temperature in our room is almost unbearable at times. The heat acts on the exmer, causing it to change chemically, and when the form is removed from the machine, some eight hours later, the liquid inside it has hardened into a tough, clear sheet of lenses. These lenses are then separated, cleaned, inspected and packed for shipping. But, let me repeat, only two people on the first shift, and my partner and I on the second, work in the bright, hot room containing the pressure-cookers.

The wall on one side of our room is thin and corrugated, and is termed a "safety wall" by the factory's Insurance Company. This means that if one of the machines explodes, instead of spewing destruction in all directions, possibly into the separating or inspection area, the force, seeking a path of least resistance, will push this wall outward, away from the rest of the building. Only two people need disappear.

The ceiling in our room is supported by a network of bare steel girders, and festooned with fiery bright floodlights. Our room is bathed in artificial brilliance. Every object in our room, the machines, the walls, the girders, ourselves, becomes unreal in the harsh glare. These lights are special Helium Arc Lamps, and when they suddenly flicker and die, which they frequently do (because the factory's generator is new and unreliable), our room is plunged into utter hot darkness. Our room has no emergency lighting system, because the styrene mixture we use is flammable. (Thus, portable radios, flashlights, matches and anything else that might cause a fire are prohibited in our work area.)

That is, the styrene is flammable only until it is poured (or inserted) into the machine. At which point its flammability becomes an asset instead of a liability. Once we've got it inside the machine, it's *supposed* to expand, though admittedly at a slower rate than it would like. This property of styrene, its desire to expand rapidly, makes it a difficult material to handle. You see, it especially wants to rebel at room temperature—to express itself pyrotechnically, so to speak. Because of this unfortunate tendency towards violence, it must be stored in a large refrigerator at one end of our room. We remove it from the freezer on a hand truck (styrene is shipped and stored in huge shiny steel drums), place it on the prongs of a fork-lift, and raise the cold drum high into the air. At the bottom of the drum is a petcock and rubber tube affair, which is attached to a Filling Machine (similar in size and shape to an eight cylinder automotive engine block). The styrene is thus gravity fed into the Filling Machine.

The Filling Machine, a massive piece of complications, is mounted on a large chain hoist, so it too can be raised or lowered. However, this process of loading the Filling Machine has not yet been perfected. We only know it's full when noxious streams of styrene splash to the concrete floor. The overflow can then be stemmed by shutting the pet-cock and lowering the forklift.

Now this Filling Machine, suspended on its chain hoist from two long overhead rails, is able to traverse the entire length of the room, enabling it to service all four of the pressure cookers. My partner pushes, while I pull it into position, slipping on the treacherously deceptive puddles of styrene as they play out behind us. The Filling Machine leaks constantly. Once we've managed to bully it into the proximity of the pressure cooker we're about to use, half of the battle is won. The other half is occupied with coupling twelve tiny translucent tubes between the two bulky inanimate objects, whilst fierce streams of styrene spray about our persons.

Styrene is possessed of strange properties.

It eats away the rubber soles of our shoes. It gobbles at bare skin. It devours eyeballs.

The barrels of styrene are clearly labelled "Non-Life-Supportive."

Which means an atmosphere of pure styrene would kill you quick. Each time I enter the freezer to remove a drum, I gag on the stench, my head spins, I almost black out, but if I'm lucky, and fast enough, I know I'll probably emerge intact, it's happened before. I usually survive.

In some ways styrene is poetic ... it has poetic qualities. Styrene is one of the ingredients in Model Airplane Cement. And Model Airplane Cement, ingested through the nostrils, can alter a person's consciousness. More than one Nirvana has been sealed by this method.

And styrene smells.

The smell gets in your clothes, your hair, everywhere. It has a very distinctive smell. People tend to avoid you. Nobody wants to make love with you. You become a pariah, an outcast, an abnormality.

But I digress. The connections are finally made, the forms inside the pressure cooker are filled, the Filling Machine is dragged away, and the switch turned on.

II.

My wife and I live in a decaying two-hundred-year-old stone farmhouse, which clings precariously to the side of a steep embankment.

It goes from three stories in the front (living room, bedroom, attic) to five stories in the rear (tool shed, kitchen, parlor-bathroom, back bedroom, attic). The size and shape of our house (it's not ours, we rent) presents us with a constant series of problems. For example, if, in the middle of the night, I want a snack, or some juice to take an aspirin with, I must descend from the front bedroom to the living room, and then from the living room to the kitchen, leaving a diagonal trail of light behind me.

If, while in the kitchen, I hear a noise in our backyard (on our mountain), I have to exit from the kitchen door onto a crumbling cement walkway, flashlight in one hand, the other groping for the rusted iron railing, and trundle carefully down a tilted flight of badly chipped steps to the slope below. Luckily (or unluckily) the bedroom is so far removed from the kitchen that it's impossible to hear anything out back.

The incline falls away so sharply that when I wander into the back bedroom to look for a book, or a magazine, or just to ponder my fate, and happen to glance, absentmindedly, out upon the world behind our house, I'm always surprised by how small—how far away—everything is. Sometimes the view exhilarates me, if things are going well, but if I'm depressed, which seems to be the case more often than not these days, it adds an even greater distance between me and any peace of mind.

From this vista, following the base of the house downward, the hill, dotted by tall clumps of twisted pine, finally flattens into a stubbly clearing, traversed by a small creek. Beyond the creek is a large field, and beyond the field a highway (which replaced the road our house fronts on). Beyond the highway is a shopping center. The shopping center is flanked by several heavily populated subdivisions.

Rising far behind this strip of activity are the same blue mountains that I can see through the steel grates that cover the side windows of the plastics factory.

I live only a couple of miles from where I work.

The interior decoration of the house was bequeathed to us by the previous tenant. The living room walls (two feet thick, that's how they built them years ago, and all solid stone) are wallpapered in a zig-zag pattern of random reds, oranges and greens. It had to take a deranged sensibility to design such a mess ... but why did the single woman with her two children who lived here before us select it for her home? God knows, she must have seen some strange corners of truth while sitting in that room watching TV.

The windows, however, are nice, as the thickness of the walls gives way to recessed sills, deep enough to sit on comfortably. The thinner walls of the parlor-bathroom, a later addition to the basic house, are papered in a silvery confection, so clearly reflective that one can watch one's self on the toilet.

The front and rear bedrooms were a shambles when we moved in, the wallpaper flaking and peeling in long discolored strips. I scraped through layers of ancient paper and paint, finally exposing the pockmarked plaster base. I sealed and painted the walls of the two rooms as best I could—but whenever it rains portions give way and crumble to the floor in small mounds of gaudy dust.

The attic is beyond help. The roof, an old slate and woodbeam type, leaks like a sieve—and the landlord says that the only way to fix it is to put on a whole new set of slates, which he can't afford to do, do we want to move? But, as the rent is dirt cheap, a hundred-and-twenty-five a month for an entire house, we say no, and stay on.

I've constructed a series of metal troughs, running them from the worst of the leaks to the eaves, where I cut a number of openings for drainage. It actually seems to work to some degree, and though the plaster walls beneath still continue to disintegrate, at least there isn't any more flooding in the bathroom or kitchen.

Just describing the physical condition of my surroundings is tiring ... but I've been avoiding the central issue ... and that is that I'm going through a terrible period in my life.

My marriage isn't working out.

My wife and I have become enemies, of a sort. She can't stand the smell of plastic I drag around with me like a shroud. The house stinks of it—my workshoes, soaked with caustic styrene, sit in the furnace room decaying into their cardboard and leather components. Unerasable black footprints have stained the kitchen floor forever. The kitchen door is the only one I'm allowed to use when returning from work. I stumble into the dark chilly kitchen after midnight, gagging on my own stench, tear off my deformed boots, throwing them in the general direction of the basement, open a beer, and try to drink myself back to sanity. Quite often I settle for gentle oblivion. Sometimes the smell is so strong in my hair, even after washing it, that I'm forced to make my bed on the living room couch, and I lie there, nursing a beer, looking at the nutty wallpaper, and think about my wife sleeping directly above me.

My wife, to save her life I suppose, has created a new lifestyle right before my eyes. She's hung beaded curtains between the doorways, and cluttered the house with broken antique furniture. Vintage movie posters stare back at me from the walls. Strange electrical appliances proliferate—juicers and blenders and canopeners and hairdryers and waterpiks and humidifiers and crock pots and so on. She works in a health food store, and takes handfuls of vitamins all the time—her purse is filled with them. Also, she's joined a spa, and I'm sure she's having an affair with her physical therapist. I'm bitter, I'm bitter, and worse, this problem is all my fault.

I'm going through a nervous breakdown. No, that's not entirely true. I'm going through a breakdown of the imagination. That is true. I have no conception of the future any more, and having no conception of the future means that I'm stuck here in an everlasting present, passively letting events flow over me like waves on the beach. I can't seem to think my way out of the dilemmas I'm faced with ... if it was one problem, or two, I might have a chance, but the job, the house, and my relationship are all tied together—and on top of everything the Arab nations have placed an oil embargo on my country. What this means in practical terms is that on a Saturday, let's say, I'm supposed to meet my wife in the city at her place of work for dinner, or a movie, if we should happen to have the extra money—but I sit in my car, in a line of cars, in a long line of very slowly moving cars, looking at my watch, feeling my stomach twist into knots, knowing that by the time I finally get two dollars of gas (because that's all they'll give) and drive into town, whatever good time we might have had will be irretrievably lost. She'll be furious. Where were you, why are you late, why didn't you plan ahead, have you been drinking? And she's right, I seem to trap myself, plan my own destruction. My wife is so much quicker than me, especially in the emotional sphere. She seems to have identified my impasse and is bailing out. While I tread water. Drinking too much. And returning day after day to a plastics factory.

IIIA.

The pillbox is a six-foot cube of concrete, surrounded by barbed wire, housing two massive freezers. Each of these freezers has its own thermostat, and each thermostat is wired to the local Wells Fargo Protective Agency. If either thermostat begins to register a rise in temperature an alarm is automatically triggered, causing a Wells Fargo employee to telephone the plant with the bad news. The reason for such an elaborate warning system is this: the freezers are used to store the exmer (which creates the chemical reaction during the pressure-cooking process) before it's mixed into each batch of styrene. And if styrene is highly flammable, the exmer alone is downright explosive (at room temperature styrene will evaporate if not constricted; the exmer will detonate violently.) However, once the frozen exmer is dropped into a barrel of styrene it dissolves, becoming much more docile, ready to perform its task. If a freezer-fail is not corrected, the pillbox and its contents would be demolished in a bright flash of sound.

Theoretically, upon receipt of such an emergency call, I must race out of the factory to the pillbox, produce a key, open the barbed-wire gate, and seek an explanation for the malfunction.

If I am unable to coax the freezer back to life with sweet reason or swift kicks, I'm supposed to speed back to the plant, locate the portable generator (which is mounted on two skids like a child's sled), drag it down to the concrete enclosure, hook it up to the wounded freezer, and start it with a lawn-mower whipcord. When the factory foreman tried to demonstrate this procedure during my training period, he couldn't get the generator going. I asked him what I should do if, just for the sake of argument, the same problem occurred during a real crisis.

"If all else don't work," he answered, "and you're out of gas or whatever, you gotta take the little buggers (the exmer is packed in small clear trays like cuts of meat in a supermarket) and throw them down towards the expressway, so the little buggers will blow up away from the plant."

Sure—I can just see myself standing on the side of the hill like some kind of crazy person pitching little meat-trays like baseballs, risking my life for three bucks an hour, while frightened drivers swerve about below, shocked by the orange puffs of smoke and concussion. Sure—I'm a sucker—I'd probably do it.

IIIB.

When the hardened sheets of plastic lenses have sufficiently cooled (they're not really cool; in fact, they're usually still hot to the touch, like toast from a toaster) they're removed from the steaming pressure-cookers and stacked on specially designed carts.

This act of removing the plastic sheets from the pressure-cookers creates a static charge; any time two materials come into contact and are separated, one assumes a positive charge and the other a negative. The sheets therefore attract copious amounts of dust and lint, like iron filings to a magnet, making them unusable. The static charge is neutralized by gently waving a two-foot-long radioactive bar back and forth above each sheet. This bar is the anti-static rod. Its radioactive core (the anti-static rod is registered with the Atomic Energy Commission—to tamper with it, or to remove it from the factory, is to commit a felony) is ionized, which means it contains extra electrons; electrons looking for a more stable environment. And the electron starved plastic sheets provide it. Making everyone happy. The electrons, the lenses, the factory owners; everyone, that is, except me. While doing its job, the rod, I fear, is also doing something else, something not so nice.

Every time I wave this magic wand over the sheets of plastic like some kind of demented tooth fairy, my white smock billowing around me with the motion, my gut tightens, my sperm die. I'm sure of it. This factory is probably making me sterile. (My wife and I don't talk about it.) And possibly, at the same time, mutating my cells, opening the genetic door to cancer, that unwelcome though ever-present guest.

IV.

No particular violence. A winter sun is high above the house, far away.

I hustle out of bed and into my clothes, shivering in the cold, and stumble down two flights of stairs to the kitchen. My wife is long gone. To her job at the health food store. Or wherever. She didn't move when I eased myself into bed after work last night, though I doubt she was asleep. She's turned into quite a good little actress lately, despite the limitations of her role.

Opening a beer, I survey our poverty pocket of a refrigerator. A few lonely leftovers working their way back to nature, sitting unwrapped on tiny chipped saucers. Butter. Brussel sprouts. Meatballs. Also, a half-finished carton of milk. And a small project of Tupperware containers filled with various unlabeled grains and powders. But I'm not about to mess with the unknown. Give me a Big Mac any day.

So I sip at my beer and stare out the kitchen window. And curse my wife because she's got the family car, which is really a truck, which means I'm stuck here until I have to leave for work. My wife and I share a GMC pick-up truck. It's pure white, with a bright red interior. We used to take turns driving it, but the overlap in our jobs (she works days, I work nights) killed that arrangement. Now she uses it almost exclusively. And I bum rides to work with my partner.

My partner's name is Arnold Sebniewski. He's a short fellow with long black hair slicked back in a glossy high-rolling pompadour. He married a young girl, a very young girl. A child-bride of sixteen. And they play house in a poor neighborhood.

Bad luck continually nips at his heels, never quite devouring him whole. His car is an antique gas-guzzler. A living fossil he can't afford. But he's in a bind. No one would buy it if he tried to sell, and he needs a means to get to work. So every day I stand on the side of the highway praying for the well-being of his junkheap, and breathe a sigh of relief when it finally heaves into view.

Arnie chain smokes. This habit (no smoking in our work space) makes him a maniac at work. He runs in and out of the pressure-cooking area all night long like a terminally nervous whirling dervish, his smock covered with ashes and cigarette burns.

And he can't see too well either. Arnold wears thick glasses that keep falling off his head to the greasy concrete floor. He picks them up and wipes them on his dirty smock, grinding oily crud into the lenses. He's effectively blind. Combine this handicap with his nicotine craving and the result is an interesting series of problems.

For example:

The forklift we use in our room to shuffle around the barrels of styrene is an electrically-controlled hand-operated affair. It's large and powerful. A useful machine. Arnie was fooling with it one night, and he managed to simultaneously start it and lock it into reverse. The forklift playfully backed him into a wall and, the handle jammed in his gut, raised him six inches from the floor. I thought he would be gored to death, while I stood there watching helplessly, a knot of fascinated fear expanding inside me.

But the machine's safety switch shut off, leaving him suspended in the air, very much alive, his tiny feet kicking about. Another time, bored by the routine of our job, he climbed up on one of the hissing pressure-cookers, reached for an exposed girder high above him, and pulled himself on top of it. He stood up slowly, a bit shaky, and grinned down at me. He then did a little victory dance to celebrate his feat, lost his footing, and fell to the floor. I couldn't believe it. I rushed over to his twisted body, expecting to find his back broken, or his neck snapped, but once again bad luck had merely tapped him on the shoulder and then departed for a while. His smock was soaked with dark patches of styrene, his hair was matted with the stuff, his eyes were closed, but he seemed intact.

I carefully lifted him from the floor, filled with a mixture of pity and disgust, and carried him to the infirmary, where I rinsed his eyes with warm water. Leaving him there, bathed in the eerie green infirmary light, I returned to our room to check the temperature levels. I didn't want the whole factory to blow up. At least not while we were in it.

Seconds later he reappeared in the room, looking no worse for the wear, an unlit cigarette dangling from the corner of his mouth.

V.

The pressure-cookers are essentially huge hot water heaters, with built-in thermostats and timers. With their lids shut they look like large rectangular stainless-steel coffins. Inside each pressure-cooker are thirteen movable cast-iron plates and a hydraulic arm that projects towards them from the right inner wall. Assembled forms are placed between the plates, and then the entire sandwich (plate, form, plate, form) is compressed by activating the hydraulic arm, making it air-tight (this keeps the styrene inside the forms and the boiling water out). The forms are filled, tiny plugs hammered into the pour holes with a rubber mallet, the water intake valve turned on, and the machine is ready to run.

The forms into which we pour the styrene are also sandwiches. The core of each form is a three-quarter-inch thick steel pattern with twenty-four convex glass inserts. An aluminum "cupcake tray" with twenty-four matching concave impressions is placed on either side of the core. Both aluminum end pieces are edged with compressible rubber gaskets. The three pieces that make up a finished form are held together with metal clamps, the same kind high-school students use to bind their term papers.

After the forms have been locked into place inside the pressure-cookers, the clamps are knocked off with a hammer and screwdriver.

The gaskets are a bitch to put on. They're made of tough white rubber that doesn't bend easily. We cut them in twelve foot lengths from a big spool, and throw them on a hot pressure-cooker (making them more pliable) until we're ready to use them. As you begin to edge an aluminum "cupcake tray" with the warm rubber your hands blister, but by the time you reach the final razor-cut (the gaskets have to be cut precisely—a mistake can ruin an entire run of twenty-four lenses) the material is cold and intractable. I've seen my partner murder a gasket with a ball-peen hammer, hitting it again and again on the floor.

After each run is completed, the forms are taken apart, the hard sheets of lenses removed, the melted gaskets pried off and thrown away, the cores vacuumed carefully, and the aluminum "cupcake trays" banged back into shape. There is often a lot of crystalline dark-brown plastic waste stuck to the various parts of the pressure-cookers, styrene that has oozed out of minute leaks and partially vaporized, partially burned. This plastic waste has to be chipped from the metal surfaces and swept up. My partner handles the cleaning chores while I wheel the lenses to the packing and inspection area.

We construct extra forms during the period of time it takes the pressure-cookers to complete their runs. We're always far ahead of the machines. The owners of the plant are continually devising new ways to collapse the time it takes to bake a batch of lenses, but we still end up with a lot of time on our hands (and the owners are not around to supervise us during the bulk of our shift). We have different ways of making the long nights at work go a little faster—my partner takes drugs and I drink.

He gets his stuff from two of his friends, both Vietnam Vets who survived the war—one was a tank commander and the other a marine. The marine stepped on a buried artillery shell one day while walking point for his squad. A booby-trap. He should have disappeared, a small pink mist dissipating over a muddy trail far away from any plastics factory. But the detonator was defective.

The explosion occurred anyway, trapped inside his brain, where it goes off periodically, and the only way he knows how to defuse it is with strong medicine—speed, acid, quaaludes.

They sneak up to the cafeteria window, commando-style, jimmy it open with a large hunting knife, and ease their way into the factory (this is the only way to bypass the Wells Fargo security system that protects the plant). We sit at a formica table in the empty cafeteria, darkness pressing against the windows, and do a variety of drugs and alcohol, mixing them with candybars and cans of soda from the vending machines.

It's usually at this point that I head for the pay phone in the hall to call my wife. I dial her number at the health food store, tell her it's me, and then hang up the receiver so she can call me back (I can only afford the initial dime it takes to reach her).

I don't know why I call her every night. We always end up arguing, but it's a ritual I adhere to faithfully. I open the conversation by asking her how she's feeling, how are things going at work, is her manager still making passes at her. And this kicks it off. (I wouldn't know that her manager makes passes at her if she hadn't told me.) To be told something like that and not be able to do anything about it (she likes the job, we need the money, so I can't interfere) ties my stomach into knots. (Maybe she likes the attention.) I pop open a beer and wait for her response.

Are you drinking on the job again, is that why you're so hostile, you don't trust me, we should get a divorce. I apologize and try to change the subject. Sometimes I'm successful on the first attempt. If I'm not, we circle around the topic of trust for a while, until it's clear to both of us that we're just repeating the same old endless, unresolvable argument. Then we move on to a discussion of our finances. How are we ever going to pay next month's rent, the truck payments, fuel bills, etc.

Somehow or other a tenuous peace is finally achieved, and we're able to end the conversation only vaguely dissatisfied (there've been times I've hung up on her in a blind fury, and there've also been times when she broke off the connection abruptly). Like a child picking at a scab on a wound we worry our relationship, but continue on.

I hang up the phone and wander back into the pressure-cooking room to check the gauges. I look at the pile of finished forms stacked on the floor, waiting their turn to be filled with styrene. The helium arc lamps are burning brightly, without a flicker. Everything in the room is normal.

I walk through the double set of doors to the inspection and packing area, past the auto-clave where the lenses are washed, over to one of the side windows. Peering through a heavy steel grate I can barely see the outline of the mountains in the distance, darker than the night.

North Main Street, Wilkes-Barre

goes like this: bar, church, funeral
home. Bar. Abandoned factory,
smokestacks. Derelict hotel.
The bus terminal is bare
and cold. The sides of the valley,
glimpsed down every street, rise like
walls. On the mountain, hidden coal
fires smoke. In the valley, the
sluggish river laps at the banks
of the levee. When it rains hard for
days, people here get nervous.

—Michael Lindgren

Zorkwad

Doug Shields

My name is Zorkwad Zlog from the planet *Gliese 581 g*. You humans discovered my planet shortly after you realized that your sun isn't the only star that harbors planets. Congratulations. But then your scientists decided that my homeworld may not exist after all. Maybe it does, and maybe it doesn't. My people await your verdict.

I am the only one of my friends who owns a spaceboat. I call it the Zorkdrive. Whenever our gaming crew runs out of Dr. Pepper or finds itself in need of an exotic multi-sided die, I'm the one who makes the trip to Earth to resupply.

Being as I own a boat, I fancy myself its captain. Calling yourself a captain counteracts the dorkiness of spending your free time drinking Dr. Pepper and rolling dice. My captain's uniform, knitted by my amazing grandmother, landed me a relationship with the rising interstellar actress known as Glissa de Gliese. Like most movie stars, she is known for a particular type of role. She often plays the girl who solves complex problems and has a technical vocabulary. You know, the hot one. The one who doesn't get laid because the other characters are either a) too stupid to realize how hot she is, or b) too stupid to be noticed by her. Usually both.

Unfortunately my relationship with Glissa isn't completely rosy. Between her dense production schedule and my frequent trips to Earth, we don't see each other often. Our playdates sometimes involve ice skating. Sometimes opera. Always Dr. Pepper. Our most recent date was the most difficult.

My gaming party was down to its last case of Dr. Pepper. Moreover, we'd reached a gaming impasse that required a 100-sided die, also known as the revered d100. I proposed that we use a pair of d10, which is functionally equivalent, but old Martin Xenophart demanded the purity of a single die, a die that cannot exist as a regular polygon and therefore must be carved from a sphere. A die that takes almost as long to come to rest as a marble. A die that is only manufactured on one planet: the planet that produces the Galaxy's favorite corn-sweetened drink, and the carbonated gaming capital of the known Universe: the planet Earth.

Human, I hope you're beginning to realize how precious your dice and Dr. Pepper are. I once bribed a Galaxy cop with a d20. I also traded a case of Dr. Pepper for an interstellar communicator. In fact, dice and Dr. Pepper have protected you from conquest. Not only have the empires agreed not to invade your defenseless little rock, but they have also effected the Treaty of Human Bliss, which forbids non-humans from informing you that alien life exists. We don't want to startle you. More importantly, we don't want you to divert your resources away from manufacturing dice and Dr. Pepper in some futile attempt to defend yourselves.

By telling you my story, I am violating the Treaty of Human Bliss. I do hope you won't tell.

I was fueling up the Zorkdrive and suiting up for the journey when I got a surprise call from Glissa. She was sobbing. The studio had pulled the funding from a movie in which she was playing a computer hacker. Her character was battling a rogue empire that, in blatant violation of the Treaty, had invaded Earth and sparked a galaxywide economic depression.

Unfortunately, the studio bowed to pressure from a banker who claimed that the villain resembled her eldest son. Now Glissa was out of a gig.

She was on her way back to *Gliese 581 g* and wanted to see me when she got here. I told her that I was about to head to Earth but I would spend a whole week with her when I got back.

She didn't see the logic in my offer. She suggested that I stay home until she could accompany me to Earth. "You know, take a trip together. Like a real couple."

"That'd be fine," I said, "except we'd be out of Dr. Pepper for two full weeks. Spizzard would go crazy. Martin Xenophart might murder someone. I don't want that kind of blood on my tentacles."

Glissa screamed the horror-movie scream that never comes out of real-life throats. A resentful pressure pushed into my chest as I agreed to delay the trip.

The gamers didn't take the news very well. Spizzard sniffled, then cried, and finally wailed. Martin Xenophart accused me of being led around by the ink squirter. I told him that he is a Dr. Pepper addict and that my girlfriend's feelings are more important than his addiction. He bit me in the third tentacle. I spat ink on him. We stung each other over and over until we were both laid out on Mom's basement carpet.

When Glissa finally arrived at Mom's basement, we wove our tentacles around one another in a moment of joy that only lovers can share. A few moments later the old resentment pushed itself back to the surface. I told Glissa that the Zorkdrive had been departure-ready for a whole week. We boarded the boat and flew between the stars in thick silence.

After driving twenty agonizing light-years, I set the Zorkdrive down in a darling suburban forest in United States, a region known for its Dr. Pepper and gaming accessories.

Glissa and I donned our human suits and looked at one another, each wearing glass eyes embedded in masks attached to body suits that would fool the local humans, assuming the humans didn't spend too much time touching us. Since we'd skimped and bought the cheaper masks, the eyes didn't quite fit. Sunglasses were therefore a necessity. We both love costumes so much we jumped at the sight of one another. I traced her artificial hand with my artificial finger. We remembered why we'd fallen in love.

Earth hadn't changed much in the decades since I'd last been here. The adolescent humans were now dressed a bit less grungy, as though they might be hoping to reproduce. Also, the race had finally developed hand-held communicators that took up their entire attention. They looked down at their communicators and even pushed buttons while they walked. They never looked at us. They didn't notice the slightly inhuman texture to our skin. They used their peripheral vision to avoid bumping into us. I suspect the next generation will evolve sonar.

We had no problem finding the cases of Dr. Pepper, but the d100 was more of a challenge. I searched the endless line of strip malls and found several gaming stores, each offering multisided dice but none carrying the one I needed. One of the nerd clerks offered to order a die for me, but I found that idea inefficient. I asked him for the address of his supplier, but he refused. I resisted the urge to spit acid in his face. Another nerd clerk suggested that I look on something called the Internet, but he had difficulty explaining exactly where the Internet was. I asked him for the address, and he simply replied, "Google knows everything."

So this became my task: to find the all-knowing Google.

Glissa, for her part, was infuriatingly happy. She cooed at how romantic it all was: the concrete, the traffic lights, the car exhaust. At one point she wanted to climb a telephone pole and make out.

The human suits are so uncomfortable I couldn't imagine how—to say nothing for why—anyone would want to make out. I kept searching for the die while she kept distracting me with demands for affection. Finally I pushed her away. "Don't you understand? The stability of my gaming crew depends on the success of this mission. Please don't talk to me until I have found the d100. Then I promise to make out with your human suit."

She shrieked a shriek that did not resemble a human sound. Tears leaked out of her eye holes and rolled out from under her sunglasses.

Truth be known, I have never liked Earth. I'd just wanted to land, find the merchandise, give the humans their easily counterfeited paper currency, and get off this polluted rock as quickly as possible. Now I couldn't find what I needed, and my self-invited girlfriend was threatening to expose our cover.

I ignored Glissa and focused on the task at hand. An hour or so later I noticed something peculiar: Glissa was gone. Whether she'd slipped away willingly, been abducted by police, fallen into a sewer, or been arrested by criminals, I couldn't say.

The shopkeepers were little help. They kept asking me to describe her. *Human female.* What color hair? *Female.* Tattoos? *No thank you.*

I stepped onto the concrete and called her name loudly enough to be heard at the adjacent strip malls. No response. This was terrible. She could be anywhere on a planet with billions of humans who wouldn't take kindly to knowing who she was. My panic intensified as I made my way back to the Zorkdrive.

The night was turning cold enough to freeze water. Glissa's suit was not a self-heating model. She was in danger.

I used the Zorkdrive communicator to scan the time-honored radio, television, and police bands for mention of her. No luck. I got desperate and searched the spectrum for other bands. There I found something extraordinary: all around me, broadcast simultaneously from ground and satellite, filling my cockpit, was exactly I needed: the mysterious Internet and its all-knowing Google.

With the help of Google, I found enough d100 to start an interstellar business. An idea filled my tentacles with dopamine: I'll enter an exclusive contract with the dice company. Every nerd in the galaxy will know my name. No more living in my mother's basement. My gaming crew will own its own party moon. Life is stellar!

Then I remembered: my girlfriend was missing. Even Google wasn't any help. I tried searching for "captured alien" and found an hour's worth of gruesome distraction. The keyword "human female" made me wish I had a human penis. But where was my girlfriend?

A dense projectile hit the skull of my human suit hard enough to dent it. The projectile bounced off the dashboard. It was the size of a human hand and roughly spherical. It was a 100-sided die.

Joy flew through my tentacles as I imagined the victory celebration that would happen when I returned to *Gliese 581 g* with a trunk full of Dr Pepper and a d100.

A second later I realized the implication of being hit with the die: someone must have thrown it. Glissa!

Her human suit was ripped at the side. Two tentacles were hanging out. Her sunglasses were gone. Her mask was twisted and there was space between her eye holes and her natural eyes. Her glass eyes were gone. She was moving slowly because of the temperature, and she reeked of the fermented grain that passes for party drink on Earth.

"Zorkwad," she said, "I want you to meet somebody." She stepped aside and revealed a second biped.

I was confused. Had she found another Gliesan who'd been stranded on Earth? If so, then his suit was unusual. It was shorter than the commercially available suits, and certainly more realistic than—

Shit. No. No. Shit. "Glissa, did you bring a human onto my boat?"

"Zorkwad, this is Zeek. He's my new boyfriend. He's amazing, and he thinks I am too." Zeek was clearly uncomfortable. I pulled off my facemask and spat ink in his face. He let out a human scream as the acid began to etch his cheek. He stumbled out the airlock.

Glissa lashed out with her stinger and injected venom into my ear. Then she stumbled out the airlock to chase her delirious boyfriend. I cried out for her. She called back that she was staying on Earth.

"But you can't stay on Earth," I called to her. "You'll crash the economy! I'll go to prison for violating the Treaty of—" It was too late. She was out of earshot.

I calculated the risks. If I let them go then I would probably never find her. On the other hand, if I was going to catch her then I needed my natural speed. I needed to take off my human suit and chase them through the forest in full nudity. Much better to risk a moment of getting caught than a lifetime of wondering whether Glissa was maintaining her cover. I took off my human suit.

Using my tentacles to slingshot from tree to tree, I had no problem overtaking Glissa's human suit, which was barely keeping up with her drunk boyfriend. My tentacles wrapped around each of their ankles and we all collapsed onto the bank of a creek.

Glissa started bawling. I started bawling. Zeek started washing the acid off his face.

"I hate you," said Glissa.

"I hate you too," I said, "but you can't stay on Earth."

"I know."

Satisfied that his face was intact, Zeek tried to pull his leg out of the grip of my tentacle. Foolish boy.

"So," I said, "what should we do with your boyfriend? Bury him in the forest?"

"Let him go," she said. "He won't tell anyone about us. Even if he does, humans are skilled at pretending we don't exist."

Zeek nodded frantically. "I won't tell."

Glissa sighed. "I'll miss his human penis, though. It gets hard on command."

"Really?" I looked at Zeek's crotch. "Penis, get hard." No effect.

"You just have to get him calm. It works. Really."

"Hey," I said. "Why don't we take him with us?"

For the first time Zeek stopped struggling. "You want to take me into space?"

I ignored him. "Glissa, we've always wanted a pet. It'll give us something to nurture together. Something to love. It'll be good for our relationship."

Zeek said, "Do you promise not to spit in my face?"

I shot Zeek a warning glare. I'm not sure whether he could read my facial expression, but he understood enough to shut his mouth.

Glissa asked me not to spit in Zeek's face. I promised. Back of the thighs maybe? We'll figure it out.

I let go of Zeek's leg. He didn't run. Glissa and I wrapped our tentacles around each other with an intensity we hadn't known since we'd first started dating. The trip home was sure to be fun.

"Human," I said, "return to the boat."

Glissa added, "and prepare to be stimulated."

The Case of Lady Sannox

by Arthur Conan Doyle

The relations between Douglas Stone and the notorious Lady Sannox were very well known both among the fashionable circles of which she was a brilliant member, and the scientific bodies which numbered him among their most illustrious confreres. There was naturally, therefore, a very widespread interest when it was announced one morning that the lady had absolutely and for ever taken the veil, and that the world would see her no more. When, at the very tail of this rumour, there came the assurance that the celebrated operating surgeon, the man of steel nerves, had been found in the morning by his valet, seated on one side of his bed, smiling pleasantly upon the universe, with both legs jammed into one side of his breeches and his great brain about as valuable as a cap full of porridge, the matter was strong enough to give quite a little thrill of interest to folk who had never hoped that their jaded nerves were capable of such a sensation.

Douglas Stone in his prime was one of the most remarkable men in England. Indeed, he could hardly be said to have ever reached his prime, for he was but nine-and-thirty at the time of this little incident. Those who knew him best were aware that famous as he was as a surgeon, he might have succeeded with even greater rapidity in any of a dozen lines of life. He could have cut his way to fame as a soldier, struggled to it as an explorer, bullied for it in the courts, or built it out of stone and iron as an engineer. He was born to be great, for he could plan what another man dare not do, and he could do what another man dare not plan. In surgery none could follow him. His nerve, his judgement, his intuition, were things apart. Again and again his knife cut away death, but grazed the very springs of life in doing it, until his assistants were as white as the patient. His energy, his audacity, his full-blooded self-confidence—does not the memory of them still linger to the south of Marylebone Road and the north of Oxford Street?

His vices were as magnificent as his virtues, and infinitely more picturesque. Large as was his income, and it was the third largest of all professional men in London, it was far beneath the luxury of his living. Deep in his complex nature lay a rich vein of sensualism, at the sport of which he placed all the prizes of his life. The eye, the ear, the touch, the palate, all were his masters. The bouquet of old vintages, the scent of rare exotics, the curves and tints of the daintiest potteries of Europe, it was to these that the quick-running stream of gold was transformed. And then there came his sudden mad passion for Lady Sannox, when a single interview with two challenging glances and a whispered word set him ablaze. She was the loveliest woman in London and the only one to him. He was one of the handsomest men in London, but not the only one to her. She had a liking for new experiences, and was gracious to most men who wooed her. It may have been cause or it may have been effect that Lord Sannox looked fifty, though he was but six-and-thirty.

He was a quiet, silent, neutral-tinted man, this lord, with thin lips and heavy eyelids, much given to gardening, and full of home-like habits. He had at one time been fond of acting, had even rented a theatre in London, and on its boards had first seen Miss Marion Dawson, to whom he had offered his hand, his title, and the third of a county. Since his marriage his early hobby had become distasteful to him. Even in private theatricals it was no longer possible to persuade him to exercise the talent which he had often showed that he possessed. He was happier with a spud and a watering-can among his orchids and chrysanthemums.

It was quite an interesting problem whether he was absolutely devoid of sense, or miserably wanting in spirit. Did he know his lady's ways and condone them, or was he a mere blind, doting fool? It was a point to be discussed over the teacups in snug little drawing-rooms, or with the aid of a cigar in the bow windows of clubs. Bitter and plain were the comments among men upon his conduct. There was but one who had a good word to say for him, and he was the most silent member in the smoking-room. He had seen him break in a horse at the University, and it seemed to have left an impression upon his mind.

But when Douglas Stone became the favourite all doubts as to Lord Sannox's knowledge or ignorance were set for ever at rest. There was no subterfuge about Stone. In his high-handed, impetuous fashion, he set all caution and discretion at defiance. The scandal became notorious. A learned body intimated that his name had been struck from the list of its vice-presidents. Two friends implored him to consider his professional credit. He cursed them all three, and spent forty guineas on a bangle to take with him to the lady. He was at her house every evening, and she drove in his carriage in the afternoons. There was not an attempt on either side to conceal their relations; but there came at last a little incident to interrupt them.

It was a dismal winter's night, very cold and gusty, with the wind whooping in the chimneys and blustering against the window-panes. A thin spatter of rain tinkled on the glass with each fresh sough of the gale, drowning for the instant the dull gurgle and drip from the eaves. Douglas Stone had finished his dinner, and sat by his fire in the study, a glass of rich port upon the malachite table at his elbow. As he raised it to his lips, he held it up against the lamplight, and watched with the eye of a connoisseur the tiny scales of beeswing which floated in its rich ruby depths. The fire, as it spurted up, threw fitful lights upon his bald, clear-cut face, with its widely-opened grey eyes, its thick and yet firm lips, and the deep, square jaw, which had something Roman in its strength and its animalism. He smiled from time to time as he nestled back in his luxurious chair. Indeed, he had a right to feel well pleased, for, against the advice of six colleagues, he had performed an operation that day of which only two cases were on record, and the result had been brilliant beyond all expectation. No other man in London would have had the daring to plan, or the skill to execute, such a heroic measure.

But he had promised Lady Sannox to see her that evening and it was already half-past eight. His hand was outstretched to the bell to order the carriage when he heard the dull thud of the knocker. An instant later there was the shuffling of feet in the hall, and the sharp closing of a door.

"A patient to see you, sir, in the consulting room," said the butler.

"About himself?"

"No, sir; I think he wants you to go out."

"It is too late," cried Douglas Stone peevishly. "I won't go."

"This is his card, sir."

The butler presented it upon the gold salver which had been given to his master by the wife of a Prime Minister.

"'Hamil Ali, Smyrna.' Hum! The fellow is a Turk, I suppose."

"Yes, sir. He seems as if he came from abroad, sir. And he's in a terrible way."

"Tut, tut! I have an engagement. I must go somewhere else. But I'll see him. Show him in here, Pim."

A few moments later the butler swung open the door and ushered in a small and decrepit man, who walked with a bent back and with the forward push of the face and blink of the eyes which goes with extreme short sight. His face was swarthy, and his hair and beard of the deepest black. In one hand he held a turban of white muslin striped with red, in the other a small chamois-leather bag.

"Good evening," said Douglas Stone, when the butler had closed the door. "You speak English, I presume?"

"Yes, sir. I am from Asia Minor, but I speak English when I speak slow."

"You wanted me to go out, I understand?"

"Yes, sir. I wanted very much that you should see my wife."

"I could come in the morning, but I have an engagement which prevents me from seeing your wife tonight."

The Turk's answer was a singular one. He pulled the string which closed the mouth of the chamois-leather bag, and poured a flood of gold on to the table.

"There are one hundred pounds there," said he, "and I promise you that it will not take you an hour. I have a cab ready at the door."

Douglas Stone glanced at his watch. An hour would not make it too late to visit Lady Sannox. He had been there later. And the fee was an extraordinarily high one. He had been pressed by his creditors lately, and he could not afford to let such a chance pass. He would go.

"What is the case?" he asked.

"Oh, it is so sad a one! So sad a one! You have not, perhaps heard of the daggers of the Almohades?"

"Never."

"Ah, they are Eastern daggers of a great age and of a singular shape, with the hilt like what you call a stirrup. I am a curiosity dealer, you understand, and that is why I have come to England from Smyrna, but next week I go back once more. Many things I brought with me, and I have a few things left, but among them, to my sorrow, is one of these daggers."

"You will remember that I have an appointment, sir," said the surgeon, with some irritation; "pray confine yourself to the necessary details."

"You will see that it is necessary. Today my wife fell down in a faint in the room in which I keep my wares, and she cut her lower lip upon this cursed dagger of Almohades."

"I see," said Douglas Stone, rising. "And you wish me to dress the wound?"

"No, no, it is worse than that."

"What then?"

"These daggers are poisoned."

"Poisoned!"

"Yes, and there is no man, East or West, who can tell now what is the poison or what the cure. But all that is known I know, for my father was in this trade before me, and we have had much to do with these poisoned weapons."

"What are the symptoms?"

"Deep sleep, and death in thirty hours."

"And you say there is no cure. Why then should you pay me this considerable fee?"

"No drug can cure, but the knife may."

"And how?"

"The poison is slow of absorption. It remains for hours in the wound."

"Washing, then, might cleanse it?"

"No more than in a snake bite. It is too subtle and too deadly."

"Excision of the wound, then?"

"That is it. If it be on the finger, take the finger off. So said my father always. But think of where this wound is, and that it is my wife. It is dreadful!"

But familiarity with such grim matters may take the finer edge from a man's sympathy. To Douglas Stone this was already an interesting case, and he brushed aside as irrelevant the feeble objections of the husband.

"It appears to be that or nothing," said he brusquely. "It is better to lose a lip than a life."

"Ah, yes, I know that you are right. Well, well, it is kismet, and it must be faced. I have the cab, and you will come with me and do this thing."

Douglas Stone took his case of bistouries from a drawer, and placed it with a roll of bandage and a compress of lint in his pocket. He must waste no more time if he were to see Lady Sannox.

"I am ready," said he, pulling on his overcoat. "Will you take a glass of wine before you go out into this cold air?"

His visitor shrank away, with a protesting hand upraised.

"You forget that I am a Mussulman, and a true follower of the Prophet," said he. "But tell me what is the bottle of green glass which you have placed in your pocket?"

"It is chloroform."

"Ah, that also is forbidden to us. It is a spirit, and we make no use of such things."

"What! You would allow your wife to go through an operation without an anaesthetic?"

"Ah! she will feel nothing, poor soul. The deep sleep has already come on, which is the first working of the poison. And then I have given her of our Smyrna opium. Come, sir, for already an hour has passed."

As they stepped out into the darkness, a sheet of rain was driven in upon their faces, and the hall lamp, which dangled from the arm of a marble Caryatid, went out with a fluff. Pim, the butler, pushed the heavy door to, straining hard with his shoulder against the wind, while the two men groped their way towards the yellow glare which showed where the cab was waiting. An instant later they were rattling upon their journey.

"Is it far?" asked Douglas Stone.

"Oh, no. We have a very little quiet place off the Euston Road."

The surgeon pressed the spring of his repeater and listened to the little tings which told him the hour. It was a quarter past nine. He calculated the distances, and the short time which it would take him to perform so trivial an operation. He ought to reach Lady Sannox by ten o'clock. Through the fogged windows he saw the blurred gas lamps dancing past, with occasionally the broader glare of a shop front. The rain was pelting and rattling upon the leathern top of the carriage, and the wheels swashed as they rolled through puddle and mud. Opposite to him the white headgear of his companion gleamed faintly through the obscurity. The surgeon felt in his pockets and arranged his needles, his ligatures and his safety-pins, that no time might be wasted when they arrived. He chafed with impatience and drummed his foot upon the floor.

But the cab slowed down at last and pulled up. In an instant Douglas Stone was out, and the Smyrna merchant's toe was at his very heel.

"You can wait," said he to the driver.

It was a mean-looking house in a narrow and sordid street. The surgeon, who knew his London well, cast a swift glance into the shadows, but there was nothing distinctive—no shop, no movement, nothing but a double line of dull, flat-faced houses, a double stretch of wet flagstones which gleamed in the lamplight, and a double rush of water in the gutters which swirled and gurgled towards the sewer gratings. The door which faced them was blotched and discoloured, and a faint light in the fan pane above, it served to show the dust and the grime which covered it. Above in one of the bedroom windows, there was a dull yellow glimmer. The merchant knocked loudly, and, as he turned his dark face towards the light, Douglas Stone could see that it was contracted with anxiety. A bolt was drawn, and an elderly woman with a taper stood in the doorway, shielding the thin flame with her gnarled hand.

"Is all well?" gasped the merchant.

"She is as you left her, sir."

"She has not spoken?"

"No, she is in a deep sleep."

The merchant closed the door, and Douglas Stone walked down the narrow passage, glancing about him in some surprise as he did so. There was no oil-cloth, no mat, no hat-rack. Deep grey dust and heavy festoons of cobwebs met his eyes everywhere. Following the old woman up the winding stair, his firm footfall echoed harshly through the silent house. There was no carpet.

The bedroom was on the second landing. Douglas Stone followed the old nurse into it, with the merchant at his heels. Here, at least, there was furniture and to spare. The floor was littered and the corners piled with Turkish cabinets, inlaid tables, coats of chain mail, strange pipes, and grotesque weapons. A single small lamp stood upon a bracket on the wall. Douglas Stone took it down, and picking his way among the lumber, walked over to a couch in the corner, on which lay a woman dressed in the Turkish fashion, with yashmak and veil. The lower part of the face was exposed, and the surgeon saw a jagged cut which zigzagged along the border of the under lip.

"You will forgive the yashmak," said the Turk. "You know our views about women in the East."

But the surgeon was not thinking about the yashmak. This was no longer a woman to him. It was a case. He stooped and examined the wound carefully.

"There are no signs of irritation," said he. "We might delay the operation until local symptoms develop."

The husband wrung his hands in uncontrollable agitation.

"Oh! sir, sir," he cried. "Do not trifle. You do not know. It is deadly. I know, and I give you my assurance that an operation is absolutely necessary. Only the knife can save her."

"And yet I am inclined to wait," said Douglas Stone.

"That is enough," the Turk cried, angrily. "Every minute is of importance, and I cannot stand here and see my wife allowed to sink. It only remains for me to give you my thanks for having come, and to call in some other surgeon before it is too late."

Douglas Stone hesitated. To refund that hundred pounds was no pleasant matter. But of course if he left the case he must return the money. And if the Turk were right and the woman died, his position before a coroner might be an embarrassing one.

"You have had personal experience of this poison?" he asked.

"I have."

"And you assure me that an operation is needful."

"I swear it by all that I hold sacred."

"The disfigurement will be frightful."

"I can understand that the mouth will not be a pretty one to kiss."

Douglas Stone turned fiercely upon the man. The speech was a brutal one. But the Turk has his own fashion of talk and of thought, and there was no time for wrangling. Douglas Stone drew a bistoury from his case, opened it and felt the keen straight edge with his forefinger. Then he held the lamp closer to the bed. Two dark eyes were gazing up at him through the slit in the yashmak. They were all iris, and the pupil was hardly to be seen.

"You have given her a very heavy dose of opium."

"Yes, she has had a good dose."

He glanced again at the dark eyes which looked straight at his own. They were dull and lustreless, but, even as he gazed, a little shifting sparkle came into them, and the lips quivered.

"She is not absolutely unconscious," said he.

"Would it not be well to use the knife while it will be painless?"

The same thought had crossed the surgeon's mind. He grasped the wounded lip with his forceps, and with two swift cuts he took out a broad V-shaped piece. The woman sprang up on the couch with a dreadful gurgling scream. Her covering was torn from her face. It was a face that he knew. In spite of that protruding upper lip and that slobber of blood, it was a face that he knew. She kept on putting her hand up to the gap and screaming. Douglas Stone sat down at the foot of the couch with his knife and his forceps. The room was whirling round, and he had felt something go like a ripping seam behind his ear. A bystander would have said that his face was the more ghastly of the two. As in a dream, or as if he had been looking at something at the play, he was conscious that the Turk's hair and beard lay upon the table, and that Lord Sannox was leaning against the wall with his hand to his side, laughing silently. The screams had died away now, and the dreadful head had dropped back again upon the pillow, but Douglas Stone still sat motionless, and Lord Sannox still chuckled quietly to himself.

"It was really very necessary for Marion, this operation," said he, "not physically, but morally, you know, morally."

Douglas Stone stooped forwards and began to play with the fringe of the coverlet. His knife tinkled down upon the ground, but he still held the forceps and something more.

"I had long intended to make a little example," said Lord Sannox, suavely. "Your note of Wednesday miscarried, and I have it here in my pocket-book. I took some pains in carrying out my idea. The wound, by the way, was from nothing more dangerous than my signet ring."

He glanced keenly at his silent companion, and cocked the small revolver which he held in his coat pocket. But Douglas Stone was still picking at the coverlet.

"You see you have kept your appointment after all," said Lord Sannox.

And at that Douglas Stone began to laugh. He laughed long and loudly. But Lord Sannox did not laugh now. Something like fear sharpened and hardened his features. He walked from the room, and he walked on tiptoe. The old woman was waiting outside.

"Attend to your mistress when she awakes," said Lord Sannox.

Then he went down to the street. The cab was at the door, and the driver raised his hand to his hat.

"John," said Lord Sannox, "you will take the doctor home first. He will want leading downstairs, I think. Tell his butler that he has been taken ill at a case."

"Very good, sir."

"Then you can take Lady Sannox home."

"And how about yourself, sir?"

"Oh, my address for the next few months will be Hotel di Roma, Venice. Just see that the letters are sent on. And tell Stevens to exhibit all the purple chrysanthemums next Monday, and to wire me the result."

A Meating of the Minds, or, Who Minds the Meat?

J. Boyett

My lover and I decided to stop using our bodies. Of course we had to keep *using* them—for things like breathing, eating, being alive—but we decided to stop using them when making love.

"Because isn't it a spiritual thing we share?" he insisted, during the talk in the course of which we finally decided to take the plunge.

"Of course it is," I said. "I couldn't go on living if I didn't believe that love had a spiritual dimension."

"It has to be more than just a *dimension,*" said Mark. "I mean, I feel *some* spiritual link with one-night stands I haven't heard from in twelve years. But if you're going to be the love of my life, then shouldn't it be a *primarily* spiritual attachment? Say, 90% of the soul, and 10% of the flesh."

"At the very least that should be the ideal." It had always bothered me, this slap of contingency. Didn't it invalidate everything, all these supposedly deep, important, eternal things, to know that they were predetermined by accidents of gender, age, nationality, orientation, species? Wasn't it absurd that I, Janet Boyett, who felt myself to be so much a creature of thought, of ethereal consciousness, should turn out to be so constrained? An inmate in a prison of meat and time?

Mark said basically the same thing, summing up with, "Let's break these shackles." He said, "It's not just for us. It's for all humanity. Because we're not just us."

A wave of something passed through me, like a non-stick mucous, and for the first time our love felt real. Impulsively I leaned in to kiss him, despite the fact that we'd just said we weren't going to do that kind of thing anymore—one last time, I told myself, making excuses. I expect that, behind the opacity of his skull, he had the same qualm, but I can't know. The gluey prehensile meats of our tongues scrubbed at each other.

Mark handled the logistics (he's very good with tools, math, etc., whereas I'm better with stuff like feelings). Over the course of that week several boxes arrived, some containing nothing fancier than plastic or metal pipes, some stocked with grandiose tinker toys, complete with joints, flywheels, pulleys, etc. Mark had a definite vision, but he tried to include me in the designing stage, so that what resulted would truly be an expression of our union. The skeleton of the resulting structure sprang up in the living room, taking control of our common space—one section intruded into the kitchen.

I know that he struggled with how to unveil the completed work to me—on the one hand it was, naturally, hard to keep its design a secret, considering that we shared a living space and that he'd solicited some input on it from me; even more than that, I think Mark felt that turning it into some big revelation at the end would make it less of a partnership between us, and would instantiate whatever ghosts of patriarchal thought-forms still flitted through the interstices of our relationship, such a revelation being reminiscent of the male hunter depositing his prize of game at the feet of the female helpmeet in exchange for sexual favors, etc., etc. At the same time, the device represented an important development for us, and it seemed wrong not to commemorate it somehow. Ideally we would have created a whole new ritual, but that's difficult to do in a social vacuum—politically I'm absolutely committed to the possibility, but Mark and I both have day jobs, plus he was so busy with actually building the thing, and we were therefore somewhat drained of creativity in the evenings. So we decided it would be acceptable to adhere to the old rituals, as long as we did so with the consciousness that we were utilizing only the form, as kind of a stopgap in lieu of the perfect world that, given time and leisure, we would complete in our spirits, and that Mark and I personally have made no little progress on, if I do say so myself.... Anyway, so it was thus that, as I was putting through the grinder a chicken my uncle had raised and given to us as a gift, Mark came to fetch me and, taking me by the hand (after I'd washed it), he led me into the common area, counselling me to duck my head as we passed the section that intruded into the kitchen, even though I'd been ducking past it for days already, and with a kind of solemn gladness raised an arm to indicate the structure that teetered through the room, and that had not changed in the twenty minutes since I had gone to the kitchen to finish de-boning the plucked chicken, except for three joints that Mark had tightened as a finishing touch.

The structure branched through the room like a crystalline lattice, except not so regular—it worried its way organically past obstacles like the loveseat and coffee table, all the way up to our really quite high ceiling—it filled the room, but we could still easily wend our way through its empty spaces. Many of its parts were moving, many were fixed. Without exchanging a word, all the while gazing at each other with love and wistfulness, Mark and I each assumed a station at far-separated points of the room. The "stations" were points at which the moving parts of the structure had been equipped with rubber molded handgrips—we used these grips to manipulate the structure—each of us yanked the grips back and forth, more or less in rhythm with each other, and in some far corner of the lattice the pipes interacted with each other in an abstraction from the sex act. Sometimes manipulating the handle caused a pipe to move back and forth through a fixed ring; sometimes it caused a ring to alternately encompass then release a stationary rod; sometimes it made a ring and rod move together in non-dominant cooperation, so that it was impossible to say which avatar was active and which passive; for certain combinations you had to use two handles, or sometimes you had to utilize one or more foot-pedals, and sometimes you had to use all four limbs, as if you were climbing onto a stationary cardio machine, and then the parts cascaded past and through each other in Busby Berkleyish routines that had no discernible reference to the prosaic anatomical specificities of sexual intercourse.

As Mark and I worked, the room was filled with the hushed whisk-whisk-whisk of the well-oiled parts. The idea was that after a certain training period we would be able to make love to each other when only one of us was in the room. I would be able to take the role of Mark and make love to myself, or vice-versa, not masturbatorily but as a vessel for whatever spiritual essence of Mark was independent from the body and hence expressible via potentially any envelope of flesh (or if we could advance far enough then theoretically that envelope need not be of flesh at all, i.e. spirits of the dead which have been known to ensoul rooms of derelict houses, rune-carved stones, trinkets which in life metonymically acquired some special significance, anything really). From that point we would be able to figure out the next step, to move even further towards the true pattern which underlies love-making, beyond all psychophysiosociosexual contingencies.

Of course, we had not arrived at the idea of the structure overnight. This was the latest step in a long struggle for spiritual liberation; there had been others.

Hallucinogenics had seemed a likely aid. We'd tried salvia, taking it in the form of an extract of one-hundred-twenty times the potency of the naturally occurring plant: partly because we thought it would get the job done faster, partly because it seemed closer to the spiritual truth of things to distance ourselves from the accidental parameters set forth by nature, that great dumb beast. We took turns ingesting as much of the smoke as we could and then observing each other through the few minutes' trance. Once the dramatic stuff was over with, as Mark and I were floating through the moderately stoned aftermath, he'd said to me, hopefully, "I think that kind of worked, don't you? We stopped perceiving our bodies, didn't we?"

I could not be so sanguinary: "I don't know if it's so much that we had less body, though," I had to say; "it was more like the whole universe became our bodies."

He stared at me, his face congealing with horror. "You mean it made things even worse," he said, not asking a question, but turning the statement over in his mind and coming to terms with it. That was the end of our stint as psychonauts.

Our pair-bonding itself was a glaring example of social and animal preprogramming, especially given its heterosexual normativity; when you factored in the closeness of our ages and socioeconomic backgrounds it became downright laughable.

So as to break through the conceptual shackles of the pair-bond, Mark and I found a swingers' group online. The orgy took place many miles outside our typical American city. After a three-hour drive during which Mark and I chatted nervously but gamely, we arrived at a new housing development, lonely on the plains and apparently unattached to anything. It was not a gated community, though it had the feeling of one. We pulled up to the gray dark quiet house, very big but only one expansive story; looking at it from outside it felt empty, but there were many cars already in the driveway or parked on the curb out front. We walked up to the front door, holding hands (having not yet resolved to stop doing such things, this being before we'd envisaged the structure and a total break with the flesh); we rang the doorbell, and, once we'd been admitted, made our introductions. During the orgy, Mark and I avoided physical contact with each other, as we'd agreed, since the whole point was to learn to make love with each other by means of other bodies. Perhaps one way to explain it is to say that we wanted to divert the effrontery of that contingency onto other bodies, saving the pure stuff for ourselves ... but what does even that mean, "selves"? Anyway, we had sex mostly in different parts of the thickly-carpeted dim room, and I let myself be carried along the currents of flesh like a chip of soap adrift at sea. At one point, when at the same time I had one penis in my vagina, one penis in my rectum, one penis in my mouth, one penis in each hand, and the penis of a man I was foot-fucking between my feet, I felt like I was drowning, and involuntarily my eye rolled around the room, snatching glimpses of Mark where he was equally busy fucking people, the sight of him like that of a distant boat periodically glimpsed by a drowning person in whose eyes the salt water frequently splashes, smearing his or her vision. The orgy had started at one in the afternoon and it was not very late when it ended, certainly not nighttime. Mark and I returned to the city without exchanging many words. The quality of the light upon the plains was yellow and shallow, as if a hollow sphere of onion skin encased the planet and all the sun's rays were filtered through it.

But all that was in the past. Now we were banking on the structure.

After weeks of manipulating the pipes and pulleys of our structure we began to weaken from exhaustion. Part of it was because of work, our long days of being bounced by the temp agencies from one office to another. Also the manipulation of the structure was itself hard physical work.

Mark's face was ashen and drawn—so well had I trained myself to shy from the flesh that I was ashamed to notice this fact. Pointing my face down and to the left, thus looking at him only obliquely, I said, "I'm a little worried about you, Mark...."

"Why?" he demanded roughly, daring me to say it was on account of the meat. We weren't touching—between us was a wall of invisible, monkish, spiritual glass.

I couldn't refer directly to his paleness. It would make a monkey of all our sacrifices, to admit to having noticed his skin that way. Instead, almost stammering, I said, "I think maybe ... maybe the structure ... manipulating it ... I mean, I love you, but I think maybe manipulating the structure is taking a toll...." Then suddenly it hit me—that the manipulation of the structure was *itself* a strenuous use of our bodies! Excitedly, seeing a solution ahead, seeing relief, I gushed: "We need to take the next step is all, honey! ... Just a little more purification, and we won't get so tired anymore.... We need to, we need to stop using the machine ... or *any* physical manifestation ... we need to each sit in a dark room ... a separate dark room ... and just be with each other in the soul ... I'll visualize you ... except, not visualize, not exactly, not do anything so tied up with the physical phenomenon of light bouncing off a surface ... but some, some spiritual shape ... except not a shape, exactly ... I'm not sure what I mean, but that's the whole point, is that we need to take some time to discover what it means ... maybe we could ... I mean, I know we don't have much money, but maybe we could rig up some sort of sensory-deprivation chambers...."

But Mark was shaking his head already, and he interrupted me: "No, no," and to my horror tears began to ooze from his eyes, teeming out from behind his lids and writhing down his face like transparent smeared maggots. His voice hitching, throat packed with undiluted spit, he said, "I need the meat, baby."

I started to cry too. "But don't you love me?" I said.

He nodded, but couldn't stop himself from saying it again: "Baby, I just need the meat."

I don't know how much of what happened next I planned—the truth is that I was so overcome with emotion that I can't remember what I was thinking—but I suddenly found myself in the kitchen, having run there, and as if it had been my intention all along I saw my hand stretch out in front of me, grabbing the freezer door and yanking it open. Inside were the thin cutlets of raw beef, free-range, that my uncle had brought over. They'd only been in the freezer about half an hour and were not yet stiff, though they were very cold—I bunched them together in my fists and ran back to the living room, where I held them out to Mark in almost a supplicating pose: "Here, here," I said, "I love you, here."

Shivering in the grip of full-body tremors, he stared at the flesh in my hands—then he snatched one of the thin leaves of meat from me so fast that I barely had warning to open my hand and release the cutlet so that it wouldn't be ripped—with the other hand he tore open his fly and savagely pulled out his dick. I stared at it, swollen and throbbing, bigger than it had ever been, or perhaps that impression derived from my long absence from it.... For the first time I understood the notion of the totem, of its divinity; for his dick quivered with its own life, it was unquestionably an entity; but it disdained the fineries of personality and intellect the way an aristocrat will step out of the bathroom and appear before his servants in an undershirt and with shaving cream still upon his face, not concerned with his cheap dignity the way a member of the petty bourgeois would be; this was, I saw, the very definition of the divine; that dick had a far less mediated relation than I to the roiling dyonisian substratum of the maya above which we mortals putter about. Mark took the cutlet, wrapped it around this god, and jerked the bloody sacrifice back and forth three times until liquid smoke issued from its nostril and, assuaged, the red wet god retired, in stately lethargy.

I fell to my knees. Emotion. My vision slimed and I knew I was crying, so I wiped at my face, leaving, as I would later see, sticky pink traces.

Mark had returned to himself, somewhat, he looked down at me, shaking his head: "Honey ... I'm sorry ... but...."

But I was already clawing at my pants, undoing the buttons. "The genitals," I said, "the genitals."

Thus began our new stage of love. What began that day so spontaneously has hardened into ritual: Mark and I crouch naked in far corners of the room, tucked in among the empty spaces of the lattice, sometimes looking at each other but sometimes not, and, each of us with a cushion of piled cold meat under our genital/rectal areas, we bounce our whole bodies like a grandfather's knee, patting our organs of generation and waste disposal against the cutlets, or mounds of ground beef, etc. In this way our love-making has pushed all the way through fleshlessness and come out on the other side, in, I have faith, a purer form.

Mark remains precious to me. At night when my mechanism demands its repose I hold his spirit in mine as I drift to sleep. But I try to be pure, and for the most part I manage to banish his face from my mind and instead cherish him—it—in the form of that ghostly kiss of cold meat against my pussy.

SUBMISSION INFO

Interested in submitting to the *Saltimbanque Review*? Well, why the hell not? Paste your submission into the body of an email and send it to saltimbanquebooks@gmail.com

Unfortunately we can't pay, except in the form of two contributor's copies.

If you want to get updates about Saltimbanque Books, please sign up for the mailing list at www.saltimbanquebooks.com

Thanks, and adios.

CONTRIBUTORS' NOTES

Heather Austin lives in North Carolina with her family. Her stories have appeared in *The Barcelona Review*, *FRiGG* and other journals.

J. Boyett is a writer and filmmaker and, coincidentally, edits the very literary journal in which his work is appearing. For information on his books and films, go to www.jboyett.net

Of all this issue's contributors, **Arthur Conan Doyle** is probably the most well-known. The tale of misogyny (with a dash of colonialism) appearing in this issue was first published in 1893.

Douglas Hahn is a poet and web developer who lives and works in San Francisco.

Brian Hurley is the Books Editor at The Rumpus and an Editor at Fiction Advocate. His writing has appeared in *The Millions*, *Electric Literature*, and *Full Stop*.

Ron Kolm is a founding member of the Unbearables and has helped edit their five anthologies. He is a contributing editor of *Sensitive Skin* magazine. Ron is the author of *The Plastic Factory*, *Divine Comedy*, *Suburban Ambush*, *Duke & Jill* and, with Jim Feast, the novel *Neo Phobe*. A new collection of his short stories, *Night Shift*, has just been published by Autonomedia. He's had work in *Flapperhouse*, *Great Weather for Media*, the *Too Much* anthology, *The Opiate* and the *Outlaw Bible of American Poetry.* He has forthcoming work in *Local Knowledge*, and he edited and introduced an Unbearables section in Alan Kaufman's recently published *Outlaw Bible of American Art*. Ron's papers were purchased by the New York University library, where they've been catalogued in the Fales Collection.

Michael Lindgren is a writer and musician whose book reviews appear regularly in the *Washington Post.* He lives in Jersey City, New Jersey.

Jon Rachmani lives and works in fear in New York City. As well as working on approximately three novels, he teaches English Literature at Hunter College.

Jean Richepin was born in 1849, in Algeria, and died in 1926 in Paris. "Mademoiselle" appeared in his collection *Cauchemars (Nightmares)*, in 1892.

Amy Roa is a writer living in Brooklyn, New York.

Doug Shields is the author of the short story collection *Benjamin Golden Devilhorns* and the lead poet for *Poetize the News: Making Sense of World Events through Poetry* on KPSQ-LP, the Pacifica Radio affiliate in Fayetteville, Arkansas. He is also a Ph.D. candidate in physics, researching the spiral structure of galaxies.

Matt Tanner grew up in North Georgia. His work has appeared at FictionAdvocate.com, where he is a contributor and art director, and at TheRumpus.net, among others. He lives in Rhode Island.

ALSO FROM SALTIMBANQUE BOOKS:

THE UNKILLABLES, by J. Boyett

Gash-Eye already thought life was hard, as the Neanderthal slave to a band of Cro-Magnons. Then zombies attacked, wiping out nearly everyone she knows and separating her from the Jaw, her half-breed son. Now she fights to keep the last remnants of her former captors alive. Meanwhile, the Jaw and his father try to survive as they maneuver the zombie-infested landscape alongside time-travelers from thirty thousand years in the future.... Destined to become a classic in the literature of Zombies vs. Cavemen.

COLD PLATE SPECIAL, by Rob Widdicombe

Jarvis Henders has finally hit the beige bottom of his beige life, his law-school dreams in shambles, and every bar singing to him to end his latest streak of sobriety. Instead of falling back off the wagon, he decides to go take his life back from the child molester who stole it. But his journey through the looking glass turns into an adventure where he's too busy trying to guess what will come at him next, to dwell on the ghosts of his past.

STEWART AND JEAN, by J. Boyett

A blind date between Stewart and Jean explodes into a confrontation from the past when Jean realizes that theirs is not a random meeting at all, but that Stewart is the brother of the man who once tried to rape her.

THE LITTLE MERMAID: A HORROR STORY, by J. Boyett

Brenna has an idyllic life with her heroic, dashing, lifeguard boyfriend Mark. She knows it's only natural that other girls should have crushes on the guy. But there's something different about the young girl he's rescued, who seemed to appear in the sea out of nowhere—a young girl with strange powers, and who will stop at nothing to have Mark for herself.

I'M YOUR MAN, by F. Sykes

It's New York in the 1990's, and every week for years Fred has cruised Port Authority for hustlers, living a double life, dreaming of the one perfect boy that he can really love. When he meets Adam, he wonders if he's found that perfect boy after all ... and even though Adam proves to be very imperfect, and very real, Fred's dream is strengthened to the point that he finds it difficult to awake.

BENJAMIN GOLDEN DEVILHORNS, by Doug Shields

A collection of stories set in a bizarre, almost believable universe: the lord of cockroaches breathes the same air as a genius teenage girl with a thing for criminals, a ruthless meat tycoon who hasn't figured out that secret gay affairs are best conducted out of town, and a telepathic bowling ball. Yes, the bowling ball breathes.

RICKY, by J. Boyett

Ricky's hoping to begin a new life upon his release from prison; but on his second day out, someone murders his sister. Determined to find her killer, but with no idea how to go about it, Ricky follows a dangerous path, led by clues that may only be in his mind.

BROTHEL, by J. Boyett

What to do for kicks if you live in a sleepy college town, and all you need to pass your courses is basic literacy? Well, you could keep up with all the popular TV shows. Or see how much alcohol you can drink without dying. Or spice things up with the occasional hump behind the bushes. And if that's not enough you could start a business....

THE VICTIM (AND OTHER SHORT PLAYS), by J. Boyett

In *The Victim,* April wants Grace to help her prosecute the guys who raped them years before. The only problem is, Grace doesn't remember things that way.... Also included:

A young man picks up a strange woman in a bar, only to realize she's no stranger after all;

An uptight socialite learns some outrageous truths about her family;

A sister stumbles upon her brother's bizarre sexual rite;

A first date ends in grotesque revelations;

A love potion proves all too effective;

A lesbian wedding is complicated when it turns out one bride's brother used to date the other bride.

www.ingramcontent.com/pod-product-compliance
Lightning Source LLC
LaVergne TN
LVHW010105110826
845155LV00028B/492

* 9 7 8 1 9 4 1 9 1 4 0 9 0 *